Starting A New Job
In A Week

Christine Harvey is an international businesswoman and leader. She has run companies in the UK, Europe, America and Asia, trained over 100,000 people in business success methods, and reached over a million through her articles, books, television, radio and conferences. Many of her followers have won awards for excellence and corporate growth after taking her courses at the Institutes of Management – in Australia, Singapore and Great Britain. She has trained the US Military in communication, motivation and leadership and served as Chair of both the London Chamber of Commerce and the Sunbelt World Trade Association in the US.

Christine's other books in this series include *Successful Selling In A Week, People Skills In A Week,* and *Personal Impact In A Week* and she has also written seven business books published in 28 languages. Her easy-to-grasp writing style and business expertise make this book a must-read for anyone who wants to catapult their career when starting their new job.

Starting A New Job In A Week

Christine Harvey

First published in Great Britain in 2014 by Hodder & Stoughton. An Hachette
UK company.

This edition published in 2016 by John Murray Learning

British Library Cataloguing in Publication Data: a catalogue record for this title is
available from the British Library.

Library of Congress Catalog Card Number: on file.

Paperback ISBN 978 1 473 ....

eBook ISBN 978 1 471 8.....
1

Haringey Libraries	
YY	
Askews & Holts	24-Mar-2017
650.1	
	3400018145

Typeset by Cenveo® Publisher Services.

Printed and bound in Great Britain by CPI Group (UK) Ltd, Croydon CR0 4YY.

John Murray Learning policy is to use papers that are natural, renewable
and recyclable products and made from wood grown in sustainable forests.
The logging and manufacturing processes are expected to conform to the
environmental regulations of the country of origin.

John Murray Learning
Carmelite House
50 Victoria Embankment
London
EC4Y 0DZ
www.hodder.co.uk

Also available
in ebook

Contents

Introduction

Why is it that we don't learn at school some of the most important things we'll need for life? These are things like how to succeed in relationships, how to read a contract for buying a home – and how to start a new job successfully. These are things we eventually glean from other people, through observation or through trial and error. The purpose of this book is to cut out the trial and error and to give you the experiences of highly successful people so that you can succeed *now*.

As A. A. Milne once said, 'Good judgement comes from experience and experience – well, that comes from poor judgement.' What I've set out to do here is to give you the wisdom gained by others over the years. By learning from their experience, you'll also be able to exercise good judgement and face whatever comes your way – with confidence, credibility and success.

I've also added my own experiences from running businesses on three continents and coaching my own employees to new levels of success. I want you to consider the workplace as not only a place to earn a living but also a place to develop your skills, talents and creativity – in short, a place to develop your true potential. By doing this, you'll also affect others in a positive way, which is important for your own growth as a leader.

In this book, we've covered the essential ingredients you'll need for succeeding in your new job. They include:

- preparing before you start
- handling day one with ease
- having great success with your boss and colleagues
- using the right attitudes (ones that get you promoted not demoted)
- planning your leadership future by halting failure
- promoting loyalty and leading change

- succeeding as a leader (handling difficult situations head on)
- reaching your goals with proper monitors and controls.

The people I've interviewed for this book are from around the world – the UK and Ireland, America, Europe and Asia. Their industries are wide-ranging, as are their areas of expertise. I thank each of them for sharing their insights and I hope you gain as much from them as I enjoyed tapping their wisdom and hearing their success stories.

The chapters of this book are organized into the days of the week, and the information and advice they contain have a practical focus. Keep pen and paper to hand as you read each day's chapter so that you can make notes when prompted. Your notes will build up into a useful set of prompts for you as you make your mark in the new job.

Wishing you every success and joy,

Christine Harvey

ChristineHarvey@ChristineHarvey.com

SUNDAY

What to do before you start

Starting a new job is an exciting opportunity. It's a time when you can reinvent your life and catapult your career.

Now that you're hired for the new position, there are certain things you can do to ensure success, even before your first day in the job. During your interview process you learned about many aspects of the new job, but not all. You'll still have plenty of questions about the company, the management, your colleagues and your new responsibilities.

There will be surprises and challenges ahead. What you do now to prepare for the first day will boost your confidence and heighten your ability.

Let's look at the list of what to do *before* day one:

- Discover more about the company.
- Review your job description and what might be expected of you.
- Decide on your career goals.
- Determine the strengths you bring to the job.
- Think of what gaps exist in your résumé.
- Master the way you'll speak about yourself.
- Decide how to overcome any special or difficult circumstances.
- Make the right first impression.

Discover more about the company

It's said that 60 per cent of your self-image is related to the job you do, so it's no wonder that the days leading up to a new job make people feel vulnerable. Your self-image in relation to the new job hasn't been formed yet.

When I started my company and left the corporate job behind, I remember sitting on a plane from London to Chicago to meet a client. I still felt allegiance to my old job and my old colleagues, because I had no experience to draw upon for my new role. Perhaps you also felt this the last time you changed jobs. The new job probably required some mental adjustment of your self-image; and the chances are that you needed time to grow into your new role.

Now on this job, you probably have some impressions about the company. Perhaps you even know it well, if you are being promoted from within. Either way, there are things you can do now to start forming your self-image in relation to the new job.

Psychologists advise that we can speed up the acclimation process in three ways. We need to visualize ourselves:

- working in the new role
- feeling comfortable in the new role
- succeeding in the new role.

The first step is to discover as much about the company and the department as you can. In preparing for day one on the job, Roy Allaway, a manager in the events industry, recommends finding out everything you can about the company and its personnel. 'I went on to Google,' he says, 'and found news stories about the company. I searched the company website for the names of the directors and read up on them. And I read every page of their website.'

He also went on to Facebook to find contacts at the company. 'Friends of friends usually know someone in the company or the industry and that will help you enormously,' he says. He had conversations with everyone who had any knowledge of the company. 'That gave me a high level of comfort even before day one rolled around,' he said.

Take a minute now to decide what resources to tap for this information.

TIP *You can find information about the company or department in a variety of places:*

* *the company's published literature and annual reports*
* *on the Internet*
* *through social media and other networks*
* *through your personal contacts.*

After you've done your research, make a note of your findings so you can refer to them once you're in the job.

Decide on your career goals

Let's look at where you want this job to lead. What goals do you have for the next steps of your career?

* If anything were possible, what would you want?
* Do you want to progress to senior management or be the CEO?
* Do you want to learn a new skill so that you can change industries?
* Do you want to sharpen your leadership or your communication skills?
* What is it exactly that you want to move towards?

Jot your goals down so that you can refer to them in the future.

Determine the strengths you bring to the job

This is easier than it sounds, even if you have little idea of what your new job requires. Simply do this. Think of three of your favourite accomplishments. They could be from a previous job, or even an accomplishment from your youth. All of them will lead you to skills and qualities that will be transferable to future positions.

1 Now list *all* the skills you used or acquired through those accomplishments. Consider things like leadership, management, monitoring, problem solving, good judgement and good decision-making, computers, mathematics and sales & marketing,

2 List the qualities you used in the achievements. Consider things like being responsible, organized, open-minded, a good communicator, enthusiastic, proactive and reliable.

3 Next, think of your job description and what you expect to be doing in your new position. Glance at your list of skills and qualities above. Which of these strengths can be transferred to the new job?

From now on, when you think of your new job, see yourself using these strengths – all the skills and qualities you highlighted above.

Think of the gaps in your résumé

Oliver Kelly, a consultant in the financial services industry, advises you to start planning your career early in the new job. 'What will your résumé or CV look like in ten years' time?' He sees people drift in their early career, not adding to their professional qualifications or leadership experience. 'It's OK to feel good about getting the new job, but look for the holes in the position compared to where you want to end up, and take steps to plug them along the way.'

As an example, he points to the possibility of creating a process you can pull together, or joining an organization for leadership. 'Maybe you've never had a chance to run a team or to give presentations. If not, find an organization like Toastmasters that you can join in order to gain those experiences. Then you'll be able to include these on your résumé, which will increase your credibility when going for the bigger job,' he says.

Think about your own career now. Where are the gaps between your current strengths and the strengths you will need for the job? You have now identified some career goals for your future. If you were to create a résumé now for your future dream job, what would it need to look like? Jot down your thoughts. Decide now what needs to be added to your arsenal of skills and strengths.

Mastering a new skill

Eoin Mulvihill of Biz By Media learned early in his career that he needed to master sales in order to succeed. It was not something he looked forward to; in fact, he dreaded it. 'So I took a job selling nationwide where I would be anonymous to my customers. Then suddenly, to my shock and horror, they decided to place me in the shopping centre of my home town! I was horrified because I knew every second passer-by and would have to try to sell to them. But then I decided to get a grip on my fear. I reasoned that, if I could sell in my home town, I could sell anywhere.'

On the first day Eoin sold nothing. 'I went home that evening and looked up the sales process on YouTube. I started practising the tips and I brainstormed loads of ideas on how to match the sales process to the product. I decided to give it my best shot and the next day I sold out of stock!'

'It's important, when you're new, not to overestimate how difficult anything can be,' Eoin advises. 'When you grab the bull by the horns, you can succeed at anything. Remember that all barriers are in the head. It's important to work through them.'

Think now about how you might fill your skills gaps in your forthcoming new job. Will the job bring those extra experiences you need? If not, can you work yourself into a position within the company to fill those gaps? Or will you need to join an outside organization to help you? Make a list of your ideas for filling those skill and strength gaps.

Master the way you'll speak about yourself

In my book *Personal Impact In A Week*, I discussed how important it is to give yourself credibility when you speak. This is not the same as boasting about yourself. The truth of the matter is that colleagues in your new job may not know anything about you. If you tell them nothing, it may take years for them to discover your accomplishments. The sooner they learn about your past successes, the higher your credibility will be.

To do this, you need to master the art of using 'credibility prefaces' when you speak. For example, let's say you want to talk about a recruitment process. Instead of just saying, 'A good way to recruit people to help with the event is...'

it's better to say, 'When I was Chairman of the xyz, we discovered that a good way to recruit people is...' (stating your point). By using the preface showing your previous role, such as 'When I was Chairman of the xyz,' they see that you have leadership expertise.

Or let's say that you want to make a point about your wealth of experience in your field. You might start like this: 'In the six years I worked in manufacturing, I learned...' (stating your point). Now they know that you have six years' manufacturing experience.

I remember a trip I made to South America with a high-profile investment group, made up of CEOs and people of independent wealth. The organizer of the group was so impressed that I had held a post as Chair of a London Chamber of Commerce that, each time he introduced the group to our overseas partners, he started with me and mentioned my former chairmanship title.

TIP *Your accomplishments lend credibility, not only to yourself but also to your new organization. If you've hidden your accomplishments before, now is the time to change that way of thinking.*

Think back to the accomplishments you listed earlier in the chapter. These accomplishments, and the positions you've held, are the ones you want people to know about.

Think of how you could preface a point you may want to make using your accomplishments and a position you have held that you want people to know about. Make notes on these for future reference.

Decide how to handle difficult circumstances

Perhaps you'll be entering a job that holds unique challenges. In that case, it's best to prepare a strategy in advance.

Meeting a challenge

Beth Walkup, a strategic planning consultant, remembers when she was hired to join a five-person executive team. It was an NGO – a non-governmental organization – with 3,300 worldwide employees based in New York. She would be the first woman to be on the executive team. The other four members had never worked with a woman at that level before. Since her four male counterparts had spent most of their careers in developing countries where women in management were in short supply, she knew that she would be a new phenomenon.

'I decided that my first approach should be to gain acceptance. I needed to get to know each of the four individually, and have them get to know me,' she said.

At each meeting she arranged, she focused on their area of expertise. 'If it was the finance director, I would talk about the short-term implications of the budget and the long-term implications on my area of fundraising, where I would be reaching out to a million donors.' She let them know about the complexity of her job as well as hearing about theirs.

She also needed to gain support from the whole organization in order to meet their funding needs. To do this, she first got the executive director's backing to organize weekly meetings at which she would set the agenda. 'I needed them to understand that success in fundraising was totally dependent on everyone, not just on me,' she said. 'How the phone was answered, how the office looked when people walked in – these were down to everyone.'

Think about your challenges now. Whatever you face today will prepare you well for the future. As a result of facing her challenges head on and overcoming them, Beth moved along in her career and was later named to a presidential committee with the title of Honorable. It's important to look positively upon your challenges as a means of developing vital skills.

What about *your* job? What special circumstances will you face? Will you be coming in from a different industry? Will you be the first minority in the job? Have you been promoted from within so that you will now be managing people who were previously at your level?

● Note down any special circumstances you might face.
● Now think of ways you might handle them.

Make the right first impression

It's time to plan ahead to make the right first impression. We are all creatures of habit. We cling to old ways and yet, if we want a different future, we have to do some things differently. Remember that first impressions are lasting impressions.

Here's the advice that resulted from a survey of highly accomplished people:

● Go beyond what's expected.
● Dress appropriately and flexibly.
● Fit into the new scene.
● Watch your personal communication.
● Don't abuse Internet time.
● Be prepared to meet everyone you can.
● Become accepted.

TIP *Make a list of the ways you can prepare now, to make the right impression on day one.*

Go beyond what's expected

'The boss is watching you from your first minute on the job,' says one executive. 'It's critically important to put your best foot forward and go beyond what is expected in the job, starting straight away. Come early and stay late – if that will impress the boss. Ask questions for sure, if you're not certain what to do.'

Dress appropriately and flexibly

'Dress for the job – slightly better than other equal employees, but not better than the boss,' advises one manager. 'You may not be sure whether to wear a suit or not on the first day. In that case, wear the suit – you can always take off the jacket and tie, scarf or jewellery if the atmosphere appears more casual.

Fit into the new scene

'When you are moving up in your career, in order to gain credibility, you should be aware of 'the norm' for that position. What was right in your old position may not be right for this job,' says one manager. 'For example, if you are entry level, be careful not to keep many of your college habits. Dressing sloppily, coming in hung-over and posting on Facebook are things you should change. You have a new circle of colleagues now and you need to be seen as one of them – not an outsider – if you want to succeed in that arena. Or if you're moving into middle or senior management, look the part that's expected.'

Watch your personal communication

'People abuse company time a lot less than they used to when times were better,' says one manager. 'People used to have more time on their hands and thought nothing of taking personal calls during work hours. But now you see more people doing their personal texting, emails and calls at lunchtime and after hours.'

Don't abuse Internet time

'Internet abuse is something to consider, too,' says one business owner. 'Put the shoe on the other foot and ask yourself this: if you saved up your money and hired employees with that money, would you want them surfing the net instead of working?' And don't think no one will see you! I once drove up to a building and saw through the window an executive playing computer poker. No doubt, if I had been his boss, I'd think that his job wasn't important to him.'

Be prepared to meet everyone you can

'Take advantage of meeting everyone you can, and making friends,' says one graduate. 'The intensive research required at university, coupled with reliance on television and technology, can make a solitary life quite tempting and this has created a chronic lack of self-confidence among graduates,' he says. 'This needs to be overcome once you're in the workforce.'

Become accepted

One executive says, 'Don't make waves straight away in the first week, unless that's what's expected of you. Be polite and accept all invitations for social time with other employees. Check out the social media for the company and for the other employees, so that you can start conversations in areas of mutual interest.'

'Everyone can succeed with the right motivation and the right self-training.'

Summary

Today we have looked at many of the ways you can prepare for success in your new job before day one.

The fact that 60 per cent of everyone's self-image is related to their job means that it's important to visualize yourself working and succeeding before you start the job. In order to do that, you'll need to discover as much as you can about the company you will be working for – from published data, the Internet and personal contacts.

You'll also need to examine your longer-term career goals, as well as the strengths you bring to the job. Then decide what gaps in your CV you can fill by means of this new position or through extra-curricular activities.

You'll also want to master the way you speak about yourself and your experience, in order to establish your credibility. If you will have difficult circumstances to deal with, decide now on your strategy for overcoming them. And, of course, do whatever is necessary to make the right first impression, because it will be a lasting impression.

SUNDAY
MONDAY
TUESDAY
WEDNESDAY
THURSDAY
FRIDAY
SATURDAY

Fact-check [answers at the back]

1. What percentage of your self-image does research show is related to the job you do?
   a) 20% ❏
   b) 40% ❏
   c) 60% ❏
   d) 80% ❏

2. Before you start day one on the job, what are some sources of more information about the company?
   a) Its published literature ❏
   b) The Internet ❏
   c) Personal contacts ❏
   d) All of the above ❏

3. In considering your longer-term career goals, there might be gaps in your CV that need to be filled in this new job. In which areas might some of those gaps be?
   a) New skills ❏
   b) Leadership ❏
   c) Communication ❏
   d) All of the above ❏

4. If you can't get all the experience you need to fill the gaps on the job, what should you do?
   a) Not worry about it ❏
   b) Wait until your next job ❏
   c) Join an organization or association that will give you professional qualifications or leadership experience ❏
   d) None of the above ❏

5. How should you identify the strengths you bring to this new job, even before you start?
   a) List three accomplishments from your past ❏
   b) List the skills acquired through these three accomplishments ❏
   c) List the qualities you engaged in these accomplishments ❏
   d) All of the above ❏

6. When you speak about a subject, what does a 'credibility preface' accomplish?
   a) It builds your credibility ❏
   b) It makes people aware of your experience ❏
   c) It gives people information they can use in recommending you ❏
   d) All of the above ❏

7. When you know you will have to overcome a special or difficult circumstance, such as being the first woman, the first minority or the first person coming into the job from outside, what should you do?
   a) Not worry about it ❏
   b) Do your best ❏
   c) Plan ahead on how to tackle it ❏
   d) Review the annual report ❏

8. Before you start, how should you plan ahead to make a good impression?
a) By going beyond what's expected ❏
b) By dressing appropriately ❏
c) By not abusing company time with personal communication ❏
d) All of the above ❏

9. If you don't know the dress code in advance, how should you prepare for day one?
a) Plan your wardrobe so that you can dress up or down as appropriate ❏
b) Wear your Sunday best ❏
c) Get ideas from magazines ❏
d) Not worry about it and be yourself ❏

10. What's the best way to deal with the people you'll meet on the job?
a) Keep your head down to show you are a good worker ❏
b) Flatter your boss incessantly ❏
c) Meet and speak with everyone you can ❏
d) Speak to as few people as possible ❏

MONDAY

Handling day one with ease

'When you've been loyal to one company for a number of years, you build a support base. It's hard then to face the first few days of loneliness in a new position,' says one manager. He remembers that feeling the first day in a new job, when there were no emails in his inbox. 'But, by the end of the second day, there were 70. It was a wonderful feeling to be back in the swim of things,' he says.

Today you'll learn how you can get into the swim of things quickly and easily. You'll find out how to:

- clarify what your job entails
- learn the company culture
- engage your 'people skills'
- learn from everyone
- step into the voids
- be prepared to be tested
- know when you'll be watched and assessed
- consider the risks of social media.

Clarify what your job entails

Do you have a clear picture of what's expected of you before your feet actually hit the ground on day one? Probably not – in fact, when executives were surveyed, they estimated that they knew only 25–40 per cent of the job before they started it, regardless of the hiring or briefing process.

'Managers are not always clear on their expectations during the job interview. After all, both sides are trying to sell to each other,' says business owner Walter Blackburn of Presenting Success, whose company helps people develop their speaking potential. 'The employer wants to make the job sound great, and the prospective employee wants to put his or her best foot forward too,' he says.

Therefore you probably have some surprises in store. Don't expect to walk in on day one knowing all that's expected of you. 'Instead, be prepared to get clarification,' says Walter. He recommends planning your questions in advance.

Here are some questions to ask that may help you clarify what's *really* expected of you:

- 'Tell me more about what's expected of me in this position.'
- 'What happens if I meet those expectations?'
- 'How much support do I get to reach those targets?'
- 'What happens if I don't meet them?'
- 'Is there a review process and, if so, what's included in it?'

TIP *Now think about your own position and list the clarification questions that will be appropriate for your job.*

Whether you are new to the company or new to a department, the situation is the same. When you have a new boss, you will need to get *more* clarification on your assignments at the beginning rather than later. 'It's better to get clarification at the outset than to wait for things to go wrong,' advises Phil Hawthorn, who runs One Step Ahead Training, specializing in people development. 'Later, when you know the boss's style and the department protocol, you'll feel in the swing of things.'

Louise Punter, Chief Executive of the Surrey Chambers of Commerce in the UK, recommends that you ask for details from your boss without feeling held back, such as 'I'd like to have 15 minutes to sit down with you to make sure what I'm doing is right and fits in with the firm.' That shows your reliability as a new employee. 'When you use that approach, any senior manager or CEO would have to stop and think and respect you for that,' Louise says. 'It's important for new employees at all levels to know why they are doing a project, and how it fits into the bigger picture.'

Here is what managers would advise new employees to do in their first week on the job:

- Ask questions. Although you were briefed somewhat in your job interview, you can't know it all. By asking questions, you show reliability.
- Take all that comes at you with a positive attitude.

Learn the company culture

'Do try to understand as much as you can in the first week,' Alan Elston advises. Alan's company, Front Man, hosts business events and keynote speeches. 'Listen, watch and learn about the culture of the company. Who started it, what's the senior management team like, is it sales-driven, creative, finance-driven? How do people move it forward?'

'You'll never understand the full breadth and scope of things during the first week, but that understanding will come. Think of the culture as an individual's personality. Is it slow and methodical, or progressive and open-minded? See how you can best fit in,' he says.

'In the first week it's important to be patient,' advises consultant Oliver Kelly. 'You don't want to stamp your personality on things right away. Instead, get a feel for how the boss and employees like things to work. There are differences in the way people like to communicate, for example. Some want it to be electronic, some want discussions, some like the traditional Monday morning meeting.'

Engage your 'people skills'

Adrian Evans, author of *Be A Job Magnet*, has spent 20 years as a headhunter in the UK. 'I've always been fascinated by high performance,' he says. 'Why do some people rise to the top and others don't, even with the same background and education?'

One of the answers lies in our interface with colleagues. He remembers two candidates he placed in a large American tech firm. They both started on the same day in similar departments. Two weeks later he took each of them to lunch to see how they were doing.

The first employee said, 'I'm finding it so hard to find my way around this business. I can't get any information from anyone.'

The second employee said, 'This organization is so easy to work with. Everyone is so helpful and forthcoming.' Then she went on to tell him how she networked with everyone she could, built up trust and did favours for them every time she could think of how to be helpful. Consequently, she had already met 10 or 12 of the main players and had access to all the information she needed. She developed high visibility as an up-and-coming employee.

'Their job function is the same,' says Adrian, 'but their mindset is different. One moves ahead, one stays in the ranks.'

Let's think of your new job. How would you rate your people skills now? Read the following table of positive and negative traits, to see whether you can recognize your strengths or weaknesses in terms of your people skills, and improve where necessary.

Rate yourself on a scale of 1–5 in the areas of listening, attitude and interest in others. The positive column shows one end of the scale and the negative column the other. Be honest!

People skill	Positive	Negative
Listening	I'm willing to hear other people's point of view, asking questions and using prompts such as 'Tell me more about that.'	I judge other people's points before they have even finished speaking.
Attitude	I display an enthusiastic attitude by using positive vocabulary.	I'm more likely to talk about the reasons why something won't work or to cite a negative example.
Interest in others	I show genuine interest in other people by initiating conversations and by listening and asking questions about their areas of interest.	I talk mostly about myself and my interests, or I don't talk at all.

If you want to succeed in life, I assure you that you need more than technical skills. You need *people* skills. The higher you want to progress, the more people skills you will need. I've learned this through my own life experiences as a business owner, consultant and author, and through interviewing thousands of successful people worldwide. It's true in *every* culture.

The other side of the coin is this. I've seen brilliant minds with brilliant educations falter in the business world. Why? It's because they lack people skills and self-control. They hit a ceiling in their career and they can't work out why. They see that they are left behind when their colleagues are promoted. Don't let this happen to you. You've studied hard and worked hard. Now, in your new job, you have a chance to reinvent yourself.

Why not do what Eoin Mulvihill did (see Sunday), and master a new skill? Like him, you can train yourself in any area to boost your performance. You could refer to my book, *People Skills In A Week,* which shows seven ways to deal with people successfully, to motivate them, and to catapult your performance. Also refer to Dale Carnegie's book of ageless wisdom, *How to Win Friends and Influence People.*

> **TIP** *A person's name is the most important sound in the universe. Memorizing names is important to your future career and friendships. And it's a skill you can learn.*

Now think of what goals you want to achieve. What can you do to develop outstanding people skills so that you can *move ahead and not stay in the ranks*? Make a list of at least three people skills goals you can think of for your situation and what steps you need to take to achieve each one.

Learn from everyone

What else can you do to be sure you start out on the right foot? Martin Hughes, a legal specialist, advises employees to be interested and to ask questions. 'One way to do this is to speak with staff members. Concentrate on the ones who look most responsible and hard working,' he says. Ask them what the company culture is like, what they enjoy about their job, what's good about the company, what could be done better. 'Show an interest in them and their opinion, and they will be forthcoming,' he advises.

Louise Punter says, 'Make a real effort to join in with the rest of the team. A good way to do this is to ask other team members what they do, and how it fits in or overlaps with what you will be doing.'

Step into the voids

Business owner Jane Donnelly advises new employees to go the extra mile. 'Give that little bit extra, perform beyond expectations, and you'll be noticed,' she says.

Jane makes a good point. Early in my career I learned a concept that proved to be enormously helpful in moving ahead. It works like this. Think of an organization as a circle on a piece of paper. Within the circle are dozens of smaller circles that represent people and their jobs. Between those circles are blank spaces. Those blank spaces represent things that need to be done but are not assigned to anyone or are not being done. Step into those places and assume the responsibility. If you want to move ahead in your career, look for these voids.

As Jane says, 'When you gain a reputation for taking responsibility, your chances of promotion increase exponentially.'

Be prepared to be tested

Tomas Conefrey owns a pharmacy and worked for a corporation before that. 'Expect to be tested when you first enter a new position,' he warns. 'Even your customers will test you.' He recounts his early days running the shop. 'People would come in without a prescription for a drug, hoping that I would supply it to them. They are testing to see if you are a soft touch,' he says.

The same thing happens in the corporate world. People will test you to see where your boundaries are. Be prepared for that. Tomas's advice is to say, 'Let me get back to you on that.' This buys you time to consider what they are asking or to check with upper management. Then be sure that you do get back to them, so that you build trust and reliability.

When people persist, which some will, you need to assert yourself. 'People might even try to bully you into things,' says Tomas. A sentence he likes using with these people is, 'I'm not comfortable with this situation.' It gets the point across without causing confrontation. You are not accusing them of anything. You're just speaking your mind.

Know when you'll be watched and assessed

What about when you are 'off duty'? As one manager warns, 'Whenever you are with your colleagues, you are never off duty. Whenever you are at a social event or anywhere in or near the building, you are being judged.' Mary Kilgannon, an analyst in the financial industry, also has this warning: 'Many a career has been ruined when guards are down.'

I remember once attending a Berkshire Hathaway shareholders meeting with prospective real-estate partners. We all went to hear Warren Buffett, one of the wealthiest investors and business owners in the world. Thousands came from all over the world to hear the wisdom of Buffett. For investors, this was the learning opportunity of a lifetime.

Most of us were glued to our chairs, taking notes and listening intently. When I saw that one of our prospective partners chose to wander around the product halls instead of listening to Buffett, I immediately changed my mind about having them as a partner. If they didn't share my values and priorities then, I knew that they wouldn't in the future either.

So know that you'll be watched and assessed when you least expect it. Remember, too, that people have long memories. Some may become your bosses later. Whatever you do and whatever you say will register with them. The circle of people you deal with now could well cross your path in the future.

For this reason, when you leave a company, even if you feel you've not been valued and have hated every minute of working there, leave on good terms. 'Give proper notice,' says Mary Kilgannon. 'Don't bad-mouth the management or ownership. It will only reflect badly on you and grow to haunt you in the future.'

TIP *Think now of ways you will be tested and assessed. Jot them down.*

Consider the risks of social media

The same is true for what you say and do in the social media world. Facebook is a prime example. Be sure that it has a positive reflection, not only of who you are today but also of who you want to become.

Be prudent with email, too. I remember more than one executive who has been disgraced and discredited by what they wrote in emails. Think before you speak, before you write and before you post. If you act professionally in every way, the sky is the limit.

TIP *Think about what areas are vulnerable in terms of your professionalism and how you can change them.*

Summary

From day one you'll need to clarify what your job entails, learn the company culture and engage your people skills. Although you learned enough in the hiring process to want to accept the position, there is still much to absorb.

Today we've outlined the questions you can ask to learn about what's expected of you, what support you'll get to reach your targets, and what happens if you do or don't reach them. Learning about the company culture includes finding out who could become your friends and allies and discovering how different people prefer to communicate.

Another area of importance from day one is engaging your people skills. You rated yourself on your willingness to hear other people's points of view, on your enthusiasm and on your level of interest in others, so that you know what you need to improve. We also alerted you to the fact that you'll need to be prepared to be tested, and that you'll be assessed when you least expect it. And, with social media, remember to project not only who you are today but also who you want to become.

SUNDAY
MONDAY
TUESDAY
WEDNESDAY
THURSDAY
FRIDAY
SATURDAY

Fact-check [answers at the back]

1. When you start on day one, it's estimated that you'll know what percentage of what's expected of you?
   a) 10–25% ❑
   b) 25–40% ❑
   c) 40–60% ❑
   d) 60–80% ❑

2. What's the main reason why you may not know all that is expected of you from the interview?
   a) The person who interviewed you didn't know ❑
   b) The job description wasn't written yet ❑
   c) The interviewer was trying to sell the job to you and vice versa ❑
   d) The company wants to test your creativity and flexibility ❑

3. When should you get clarification on what your job entails?
   a) When you are facing your first problem ❑
   b) When the boss is having a break ❑
   c) At the outset ❑
   d) After a couple of months ❑

4. To clarify your job on day one, what would be a good question to ask?
   a) 'Tell me more about what's expected of me in this position.' ❑
   b) 'What happens if I meet those expectations?' ❑
   c) 'Is there a review process and what's included in it?' ❑
   d) All of the above ❑

5. What will the boss think about you if you clarify what is expected of you?
   a) That you are worthy of respect ❑
   b) That you are naïve ❑
   c) That you need help ❑
   d) None of the above ❑

6. What would be the only reason for stamping your personality on things and making changes in the first week?
   a) Things are really bad ❑
   b) Your colleagues beg you to do it ❑
   c) You were brought in to do it ❑
   d) You can't hold back ❑

7. Reflecting on what you've learned at the end of day one, what are some good questions to ask yourself?
   a) What did I learn about the job? ❑
   b) Who did I meet who could become a friend or an ally? ❑
   c) How does the boss like to communicate? ❑
   d) All of the above ❑

8. In what areas might you want to improve your people skills?
   a) Listening to other people's points of view ❑
   b) Using enthusiasm and a positive vocabulary ❑
   c) Showing genuine interest in others by asking pertinent questions ❑
   d) All of the above ❑

9. When should you be prepared to be assessed?
a) On the job ❏
b) At company and non-company events ❏
c) On Facebook and social media ❏
d) All of the above ❏

10. What should everything that's posted on your social media do?
a) Make a positive impression ❏
b) Not discredit you ❏
c) Reflect not only who you are today but who you want to become ❏
d) All of the above ❏

SUNDAY
MONDAY
TUESDAY
WEDNESDAY
THURSDAY
FRIDAY
SATURDAY

TUESDAY

Succeeding with your boss

Starting to work for a new boss is like peering into a dark cave. You won't see much in there at first but, as you get used to it, more and more will come to light.

Today you'll find out how to gain insight faster, to feel comfortable faster, and to maximize your effectiveness *quickly* when dealing with your boss. In short, you'll get started on the right foot! You owe it to yourself.

In this chapter you will learn how to:

- understand your new boss
- ask for guidance without losing face
- head off problems
- be your own advocate
- decide when to offer your suggestions for improvement
- know the right and wrong times to take the initiative.

Understand your new boss

The chances are that your new boss will be nothing like the last. It's also likely that you became accustomed to working with the old boss, and now you'll need to get used to new ways. Let's look at how to speed up the process so that you will become more comfortable and effective.

We need to gain understanding through questions and observation. 'It's essential to know what's important to your employer. Is it accuracy, honesty, meeting deadlines, or what?' says one employee. 'You want to be flexible and get in sync with the new culture, while still maintaining your own ethics,' he says.

'Even if you know your job description, you can't know all that your new boss has in mind,' says Laurie Erskine who has worked in three diverse industries, from engineering to travel to teaching. 'In your first week, your boss will get a pretty good idea of what kind of worker you are,' she says. 'Likewise, you'll have to observe and get to know your boss's management style and priorities.'

If after a week, you realize that the things you're doing are not on the job description, Laurie advises the following: 'Take your boss aside and say, "I understood from my job interview that I would be doing these duties and, so far this week, I've been doing something else. Can you tell me more about your expectations?" In this way you'll clear up any misconceptions on either side. And you won't run the risk of thinking that the boss doesn't think you're up to the job.'

It's a good idea to get feedback along the way, even when you think you're doing well. Sometimes bosses are reluctant to offer suggestions for improvement to good employees for fear of demotivating them. Business owner Evelyn Cochran of Waterloo House says, 'Remember that it's OK to ask your boss for feedback. By telling your boss, "I'd like to know how I'm doing", you'll be helping yourself and your boss at the same time.'

'Remember that it's OK to ask your boss for feedback.'

Ask for guidance without losing face

Many people are afraid to ask how the boss wants something done, because they don't want to look inadequate. Don't let this happen to you. Instead, learn the *right* way to ask, which is something much more likely to enhance than damage your career.

Early in my career, I was marketing manager for two divisions of a UK company, and I reported to the managing director. One day he came into my office and said, 'The vice president just called from the US. He wants to come over and look at other companies we can acquire. Can you prepare a report, with suggestions of which companies to consider, by the end of next month?' Then he paused and walked out.

That was it. No more guidance, no more information. I sat back and thought about it. How far was I to take my investigation? Was I just to get a list of competitors, was I to research them, or was I to find out how open they were to being acquired?

I felt a huge weight on my shoulders. At first I was reluctant to ask the MD for more information. After all, I didn't want to look as though I'd never done this sort of thing before! After a few days I came to my senses and realized that very few people are specialists in acquisition. For all I knew, perhaps my boss was as clueless as I was about what the VP expected.

The next day I went into his office and asked him this question: 'Did the vice president tell you how far we were to take the investigation?' Here was his answer. 'No he didn't. Why don't you call and ask him?' It was as simple as that. Once I knew what was expected, it was plain sailing!

> **TIP** *The next time you are faced with a new assignment, get all the information you can. Don't be timid about asking. If you are, you could waste time and effort doing something totally different from what's expected of you.*

Realize that each individual has different expectations – bosses too. In business, it's not enough to do the job well in our own eyes; we need to find out what is expected first and then strive to meet those expectations. In doing so, we learn new methods and our skill level improves.

There are numerous questions you can ask that let you save face while getting the information. For example, you could say, 'Here's how I am thinking of approaching this. How do you see it?' or 'I have some ideas, but I'd like to hear your expectations before I proceed.'

'It doesn't hurt to remember that most managers want employees to do things as they do them,' says trainer Walter Blackburn. He suggests the following when you're not sure how to handle something and you still want to make a favourable impression. Think about what works best for you.

Questions that save face

1 'How do you visualize this report – a one-page summary, five pages with summary, or something else?'
2 'Is there an outstanding example that can serve as a model for what you're looking for?'

3 'I was thinking of approaching it this way. How do you see it?'
4 'I have some ideas, but I'd like your input before I start.'
5 'I have a decision to make, and I see three options, X, Y, and Z. First I wanted to check with you and get your thinking.'

By asking such questions, you show conscientiousness. Your manager can then comment and correct your course, thus averting a potential disaster. And you'll learn a lot about how he or she thinks, building trust in the process.

When things go wrong

As headhunter Adrian Evans says, 'Make sure that you know the expectations of your boss about your performance, and if they are out of line with your thinking or ability, tackle the issue head on. Perhaps you need training in a certain area, or perhaps your boss needs to be shown what's possible and what's not. Thus you are making sure expectations are managed properly.'

Dr Liz Lee-Kelley of the Cranfield School of Management teaches project management in the areas of oil, gas and defence. When faced with people who are resistant to new ideas, she's had success by showing scenarios that work, while keeping things positive. 'You may have to get around prejudices and mindsets,' she says. 'If people insist things didn't work when tried years ago, it might be necessary to set up scenarios for them to see possibilities in a modern context, and why it didn't work last time.'

What if your boss takes credit for your work? According to trainer Phil Hawthorn of One Step Ahead, which specializes in people development, you need to know your own core values so you can stick to them in your job. 'Core values include giving credit where credit is due,' he says. 'If people take credit for your ideas, you should confront them on it,' advises Phil. As an example, you might say, 'I'd like to have a piece of the credit, boss.'

Meeting a problem head on

What if your boss talks more than listens? Alison Andrews remembers a boss who insisted on daily meetings, and talked for 28 of the 30 minutes each time. 'The staff members were frustrated because they didn't have an opportunity to give their input on important issues,' she said. 'We also felt that the boss didn't value our input as no time was allocated for it.'

Here's what Alison did. She made an appointment with the boss and said, 'I have some ideas for improvements, which we never have time to talk about.' Then she explained her ideas. The boss was surprised as she thought everything was running well and was unaware of any issues. She knew that people were frustrated but not why. Alison told her the following:

- Every staff member needs to communicate.
- The meeting should allow time for each person to bring up issues, as there is no other time to communicate.

The boss made the necessary changes and everything ran well after that. Alison's frustration lifted because her points were heard, taken seriously, and given action.

Whatever your reason for frustration, remember that most bosses try their best. To resolve a problem amicably, it's often best to assume that your boss may be unaware of it. That will help you moderate your frustration when you discuss it.

Be your own advocate

What's the moral of that story? 'Nobody will be your advocate except you,' says Alison. Most problems can be solved with good communication. The next time you are faced with frustration, think of Alison's experience. 'What was so obvious to me and my colleagues was not even thought about by our boss,' she says. Therefore it's important to clear these things up as soon as possible.

'To avoid frustration, you need to know your own strengths and make sure they are being utilized,' she says. Her advice for approaching similar problems is this:

1 Write down why you're frustrated and the points you want changed.
2 Think of how these changes will improve the situation and keep a note of these to refer to.
3 Before you go into a meeting to discuss the problem, remember your options. For example, you could change jobs if no improvements are made.

'It's liberating to acknowledge your options before going into a meeting where you are advocating changes,' says Alison.

Think about your situation now. Are there any changes that you think might need to be made?

Talking to your boss about making changes

1 Give your boss the benefit of the doubt when discussing the issue.
2 Write down why you are frustrated in advance – get clarity.
3 Write down the points that you want changed and how that will help the organization.
4 Ask that the points for change be considered if at all possible.
5 Remember your personal options in case the changes are not made.

What if you're faced with an incompetent manager? 'The best way to handle it is to self-manage,' advises Mary Kilgannon. 'Don't expect help from a manager who can't deal with the job,' she says. 'Just because someone is good with balance sheets or has an advanced degree doesn't mean he or she will be good at managing people, especially in the beginning,' she says.

Here's how Mary handled it. If she had scheduling issues, she would go directly to the person involved and set the timetable. If she had problems with another employee, she would go directly to that person to deal with it instead of expecting the boss to handle it. And keeping your boss in the picture will help, while he or she is getting their management feet wet.

Ask yourself the following questions about your own situation:

- What issues might I need to discuss now or in the future with my boss?
- What steps from the lists above might I use?
- What other ideas might I use?

Decide when to offer ideas for improvement

'You may be a keen observer and a great ideas person, but there is a time and a place for offering your ideas for improvement,' says Oliver Kelly. 'If you show that you are prepared to do things their way in the beginning, they'll be more likely to accept your ideas later.'

One business owner recommends that you wait until you understand the company before offering suggestions. 'There's nothing worse than having a new employee or manager come in with an attitude of "knowing everything" and telling the boss with 20 years' experience what to do,' she says. 'It's not popular with the other employees either.'

Instead, she suggests keeping an open mind, listening carefully, and doing your best. 'More and more clarity will come as you get to know the company,' she says. 'Then your ideas will be taken seriously.'

Sometimes companies don't want your ideas at all. 'I was in an entry-level position in a big company, and when I spoke up a few times I was told to be quiet. What I came to realize is that there is no way I can influence a big company at my level,' said Stefan Fludger, an enthusiastic student. Instead, he has learned to perfect his way of doing things according to company policy, and get job satisfaction from his improved skills.

'I like my job better this way, and I'm less frustrated. And I know I won't be here for ever. Now I focus on what I can learn, knowing that things like communication and skills in handling customers will be transferable to jobs later,' says Stefan.

Know when to take the initiative

As I mentioned in the Introduction, English author A. A. Milne once said, 'Good judgement comes from experience and experience – well, that comes from poor judgement.' That's humorous in one respect, but we know that poor judgement can in reality be a disaster. Your job is to decide when – and when not – to use your initiative. Initiative can often lead to you being promoted, as long as you use it within the correct parameters. What most managers prefer is for people to take the initiative after asking for approval. By asking, you can prevent disaster.

You might say, for example, 'I have this idea, and I'd like to try it. Do you see any reason not to?' Business owner Virginia Dowd suggests that, 'After you learn the ropes, your employer may allow you to take more initiative.'

However, she remembers one new employee who took it upon herself to make a consignment sale, knowing that the agent wouldn't pay until he resold the goods. She thought that Virginia would be happy to have the order, so she didn't ask permission. 'The employee crossed the line by not enquiring about my policy before assuming responsibility,' points out Virginia. 'And sadly, as expected, the bill was never paid and the goods were never recovered.'

Walter Blackburn recounts a negative experience he had with a new employee, John, who failed to ask enough questions. John wanted to make a big impression on his boss by bringing in more money. So, on his own initiative, he decided to raise the prices for services to a long-time client company. The company was outraged. They called Walter but nothing could be done to restore their confidence. The business was lost and John needed to look for a new job.

Jean Morgan Bryant runs a company in the UK and has won a Queen's Award for export. She remembers when one new employee misquoted the shipping costs to a customer in Dubai by confusing weight with volume. 'The costs were ten times what he had quoted the client,' she said, 'and our company had to bear that cost.' Although he eventually grew to be a reliable employee for Jean, he could have been fired in a less tolerant environment. It would have been better for him to double-check when he was inexperienced.

TIP *When you're new to a job, it's always important to ask before taking the initiative, even when you're in a senior position. Think: if your action could adversely affect your customer, your colleagues or your company, then you must ask before taking that action.*

There are times, however, when you are solely responsible, that you must take the initiative without asking.

Taking a lead

Colette Johnson of Learning Curve does freelance work for a training company and has her own clients as well. She remembers once being hired to deliver three consecutive trainings on the subject of telephone sales. The first two trainings went well, but the third training was attended by a mixed bag of employees with no interest in or need for the subject.

So what did Colette do? She used her initiative to solve the problem. 'Sometimes we have to be like magicians and pull things from a hat when needed,' she says. She quickly concocted a survey for all the attendees. She asked them this question: 'If you had to spend a day in communication training, what would you find most useful?' Then she gave them a list of communication subjects that she was prepared to teach. After the survey, she launched into those subjects chosen by her delegates. The training went beautifully, and one attendee even wrote to the company with praise for her initiative and impromptu abilities.

Using initiative when you have total responsibility is different from using initiative when you are an employee. Colette, for example, was in a situation where she had to save the day. She had all the responsibility on her shoulders. She didn't need to ask anyone whether to use her initiative: it was expected of her.

Let's think about your situation. How do you know when to take the initiative and when not to? The key question to ask yourself is this: 'Will this action result in some harm to the company, the customer or employees?' If the answer is possibly yes, then it's necessary to ask before taking the initiative.

Summary

Getting started on the right foot with your boss is essential. Today we looked at ways in which you can clarify what's expected of you and how to ask for guidance without losing face. Questions such as 'How do you visualize this process?' or 'I'd like your input before starting' allow you to see what's in your boss's mind before barking up the wrong tree.

We also looked at what might go wrong in dealing with your boss and how to handle it most effectively, such as managing expectations and having your needs met.

Remember that it's important to be your own advocate. Most problems can be solved with good communication and by dealing with them head on, giving your boss the benefit of the doubt unless proven otherwise.

Of course, you may want to offer suggestions for improvement and take the initiative. If you do, it's essential to decide on the right time and place for doing so. If you're unsure, ask, and consider whether the action will result in any harm to the company, the employees or the customers.

SUNDAY
MONDAY
TUESDAY
WEDNESDAY
THURSDAY
FRIDAY
SATURDAY

Fact-check [answers at the back]

1. Why do we need to assess the boss's management style through questions and observation as soon as possible?
   a) So we can kick back and relax ❏
   b) To become comfortable and effective ❏
   c) To be able to talk about the boss with our colleagues ❏
   d) To compare the new boss to your old one ❏

2. What is the biggest reason for hesitating to ask the boss how they want things done?
   a) We don't want to look inadequate ❏
   b) We want to look good to our colleagues ❏
   c) We think they know best ❏
   d) We don't want to bother ❏

3. What are good clarification questions to ask and let you save face?
   a) 'I was thinking of approaching it this way. How do you see it?' ❏
   b) 'I have some ideas, but I'd like your input before I start.' ❏
   c) 'I have a decision to make, and I see three options. First I wanted to get your thinking.' ❏
   d) All of the above ❏

4. After the first few days, if you're not doing what you thought the job entailed, what should you do?
   a) Ignore it and get on with the job ❏
   b) Take the boss aside and discuss your and their expectations ❏
   c) Ask your colleagues what they think ❏
   d) Hand in your resignation ❏

5. What should you do when your boss is being ineffective beyond tolerance?
   a) Talk to your colleagues and make a case against the boss ❏
   b) Make an appointment with the boss to talk about the problems and make requests for improvement ❏
   c) Quit ❏
   d) Complain to all and sundry ❏

6. When things go wrong, what should you do?
   a) Be your own advocate, and do what needs to be done to uphold your values ❏
   b) Remember to give your boss the benefit of the doubt until proven otherwise ❏
   c) Remember that most problems can be solved with good communication ❏
   d) All of the above ❏

7. When talking with your boss about changes that need to be made, which of the following will help you?
a) Writing down why you are frustrated, to get clarity ❏
b) Writing down the points you want changed and how this will help the organization ❏
c) Remembering your personal options, such as changing jobs, in case the changes are not made ❏
d) All of the above ❏

8. When should you offer suggestions for improvement?
a) On your first day, to make a good impression ❏
b) After you've been there long enough to know what's going on and be trusted and accepted ❏
c) After you get allies ❏
d) None of the above ❏

9. When deciding whether to take the initiative, what should you ask yourself?
a) Will this make me look good? ❏
b) Will this harm the company, employees or customers in any way? ❏
c) Will this help me gain experience? ❏
d) Will this help me get a pay increase? ❏

10. When in doubt about using your initiative, what is the best thing to do?
a) Ask first ❏
b) Act first ❏
c) Forget the whole thing ❏
d) Ask colleagues for their opinions ❏

WEDNESDAY

The ten attitudes that can get you promoted

Do you ever wonder why some people get promoted while others don't? This happens even when they have the same background and education. Often there are attitude issues that hold people back – and often they are unaware of them.

Conversely, having winning attitudes can reduce stress and increase your chances of success and promotion.

Today you will learn how to rate yourself in the ten key areas of attitude that could propel your career or hold you back. Then you will find out how to focus on improvements where necessary. These attitudes are:

- your openness to suggestions
- how you view your importance to your company's success
- your motivation to do what needs to be done
- your willingness to train yourself
- how you deal with authority
- your honesty and integrity
- your level of self-control
- your attitude to fear and intimidation
- your level of arrogance
- your view of back-stabbing.

Test your attitudes

Whether you are just starting out or aspiring to senior management, your attitudes are always going to be of paramount importance. While your education, skills and abilities are all clearly valuable assets, your career will be severely limited if your attitudes are not top-notch.

Let's start with a self-assessment. Rate yourself in the following areas before you read on. Then read ahead and see what tips you can pick up from the expert advice of managers and business owners. By examining these areas of your personality and improving them where necessary, you will be able to start off on the right foot and increase your chances of career promotion and satisfaction.

On a scale of 1–10, assess your answers to the following questions and check whether you think there is room for improvement:

- Are you open to suggestions from others?
- Do you consider yourself vital to your company's success?
- Are you willing to do what needs to be done?
- Do you have a 'train yourself' attitude?
- Do you have a positive attitude towards authority?
- Are honesty and integrity important to you?
- Is your level of self-control high?
- Do you handle fear and intimidation well?
- Do you try to show respect rather than arrogance?
- Do you reject back-stabbing?

Keep your ratings in mind as you read ahead and plan ways to increase them.

Are you open to suggestions from others?

Elizabeth Carter was managing director of several successful businesses with international clients. When she hired Roger, she had high expectations. He appeared professional and had experience in preparing bids, which was to be his job. All looked rosy in the beginning. She didn't micro-manage; after all, he was a professional. However, after a few months, things looked less optimistic. When they had won only one bid instead of the dozen her company had expected, she spoke with him about it. His reaction was one of push back.

After seeing his presentations and bids, she realized that he had no understanding of sales or how to present the benefits of their services. When she tried to advise him, his attitude was one of arrogance rather than being open to suggestions. Before long, he was fired. 'It's a pity,' she said. 'Had he been open to suggestions, open to understanding the sales process, or had he even read a book about sales, he would still be here today.'

Contrast that to the attitude of Sharon, one of Elizabeth's best employees. Sharon was hired as a personal assistant and quickly moved up the ranks. She was always on the lookout for ways she could contribute. When her assignments were finished, she would ask, 'How else can I help?'

'She was always willing to change things to get them right, no matter how many versions of reports were necessary,' says Elizabeth. Compare that to Roger's reluctance even to let his work be seen by the managing director! Is there any wonder Sharon was promoted and he was fired?

Do you consider yourself vital to your company's success?

Whereas Roger refused to believe that his job affected the bottom line, Sharon knew that her contribution could help the company grow. She went out of her way to adapt her working methods to those of the boss by asking questions about how she wanted things done. Roger, on the other hand, expected his managing director to adapt her methodology to his, despite the fact that he wasn't getting results.

If Roger had considered himself a vital part of the company's success instead of giving his ego priority, he would have learned about sales and been open to suggestions.

This example illustrates that, if you want to succeed in your new job, you need to:

- have an attitude of eagerness to discover the boss's point of view
- be open to suggestions
- acknowledge that your job affects the bottom line.

TIP *Whether you are an assistant or a top executive, see yourself as a vital part of your company's success.*

Are you willing to do what needs to be done?

If you want to succeed, don't do what one of my employees did. I left our office in Brussels for an overseas business trip and asked him to cover a new area for me while I was away. Despite his light workload, he refused to be supportive. His response was, 'Sorry, that's not part of my job description.'

Needless to say, he did not remain part of our team. While that employee had potential, his attitude held him back. Like Roger, he wanted to do things his way, not the boss's way. They both stuck to their guns but lost their jobs in the process. Their attitude and unwillingness held them back.

One team leader in an engineering company summed it up well when he said, 'Listen closely and be willing to ask questions. Ask for more to do if you run out of things to do, and be willing to help with everything.'

If you want to succeed, have a willing attitude.

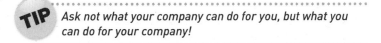

TIP *Ask not what your company can do for you, but what you can do for your company!*

Do you have a 'train yourself' attitude?

Alice has been with the same hotel restaurant for 14 years. 'On my first day on the job I was clueless,' she says, 'so I watched and listened and asked a few questions.'

Each evening on her return home, she reviewed what she had learned that day: where everything went, what time things happened, and what customers asked for. She asked questions about each step of preparation – not when her colleagues were busy, but when things were slow. 'Soon I was made assistant chef. I think my willingness to learn has kept me here longer than any other employee,' she says.

One executive advocates the same technique that Alice describes when starting a new job. 'You can't remember everything,' he says, 'so sit down each night in your first week and write down the important things you need to remember.'

Through this process you might discover areas of training you'll need. If you want to advance your career, you may want to branch out and learn better management or communication. Pippa Lee, trainer and owner of Lifecollege.org, recommends getting training in speaking. 'Most people are more afraid of speaking than dying, so you'll have an edge if you are comfortable and confident when speaking to small groups and at meetings,' she says. This will raise your profile and promotional chances.

Do you have a positive attitude towards authority?

Jean Morgan Bryant says, 'Always listen to advice, and respect older colleagues and bosses – they are trying to help you avoid some of the mistakes they made in their youth.'

What Dominic Fludger discovered early in his retail career bears this out. He noticed that some of his young colleagues had authority issues. 'If they were moved from one task to a second task they didn't like, they often did a poor job on purpose, thinking that they would get moved back to their first task. I found that odd,' said Dominic. 'I guess they didn't realize that the authorities are paying their wages!'

Virginia Dowd recounts numerous employees and contractors who didn't make the grade for this reason. 'Some people have an attitude of wanting to do things their way, even if it's not what the boss has ordered.' She says that if respect for authority is an issue, you'll have a hard time in your profession, unless you change your way of looking at it.

Do you have authority issues?

When a person asks you to do something, do you often respond in any of the following ways?

- I feel angry.
- I think I don't have time.
- I often wonder 'why me?'

Answering yes to all three indicates the possibility of authority issues.

Are honesty and integrity important to you?

For a pharmacist, lack of accuracy is a life-and-death issue. Lindsay Jefferys remembers a dispensing assistant who worked at the speed of light, but her speed caused mistakes.

When Lindsay brought it to her attention, she retorted, 'I never make mistakes when the other pharmacists are here.' She wouldn't admit her errors. Don't let this happen to you. When something is brought to your attention, be gracious and grateful for the input. As one psychologist said, 'There's a grain of truth in everything.'

To win respect, use honesty and integrity with yourself and with others.

On Sunday we talked about Eoin Mulvihill, who overcame his fear of selling. Today Eoin runs his own business, and he recently won a contract to represent an important foreign company throughout the nation. 'In the interview, I was asked questions that revealed some inexperience in certain areas. I chose to answer honestly,' says Eoin. According to the company director who granted the contract, they valued his integrity and honesty over his experience. Without honesty and integrity, there is no trust.

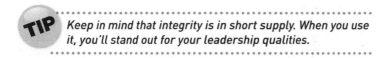

TIP *Keep in mind that integrity is in short supply. When you use it, you'll stand out for your leadership qualities.*

Is your level of self-control high?

Claire Ayres, a UK appraiser in the antiques field, attributes one of her worst management experiences to a moody employee. 'The head porter in our sales room reported to me and his mood swings were horrid! I never knew what to expect from him.' Claire's experience is not unusual. To gain respect and trust, we need to learn to control ourselves – always and every time, regardless of circumstances. There are no excuses.

What about temper? I remember a TV competition between two top chefs who were to be judged on the taste and presentation of 12 biscuits. Both were given presentation boxes. The problem was that the biscuits were too large for all of them to fit into the box. One chef put in ten, and placed the other two on top. They looked gorgeous. The other chef did an amazing thing. He lost his temper under the pressure and slammed them all into the box, banging it with his fist in anger. This was too bad, because he had won the taste test. But his lack of self-control cost him the prize.

The same is true in the corporate world. You may have the superior knowledge and skills, but you'll lose your promotion, and maybe even your job, to a less qualified colleague if your self-control is an issue.

Remember this. It's easy to maintain your control when there's no pressure. The real test is when you're under pressure. Here's how to manage it.

'Normally we can recognize negative feelings coming along by noticing our body tensing up,' says one well-respected manager who has dealt with this herself. 'Use this easy method if something is bothering you, known as HALT. Just stop everything and ask yourself: Am I hungry, angry, lonely or tired? This helps us learn what triggers our moods, or negative thinking, so we can more easily stop it.'

'Developing self-discipline and control is the road to self-respect,' says Virginia Dowd. 'Look at it this way,' she says. 'If you know what you can count on from yourself, then you know what you can value and respect in yourself.'

TIP *Developing self-control is the road to self-respect.*

Do you handle fear and intimidation well?

Would you want to work for a manager who is fearful of doing what needs to be done? Probably not. One of the leadership traits you'll need is the ability to confront head on whatever comes at you. Here are some ways to do this.

First, remember that putting yourself in the situation that intimidates you will increase your comfort level. Usually six exposures will be enough.

Secondly, remember that your thoughts can create physical stress. Researcher Edel McGlanaghy likens fear of the first day on a new job to that of public speaking. 'Our bodies react to threat,' says Edel. 'When stressed, our thoughts, feelings and behaviour tell our body to prepare for fight or flight, which can narrow our arteries and affect our blood flow.'

When that happens our thinking is restricted. To overcome that, Edel recommends the following: 'Drinking water slowly and calmly will help, as well as breathing deeply and slowly. These both slow down the racing heart.'

Next, Edel recommends reframing. 'You can tell yourself that you are really excited instead of fearful, and the same sensations that cause you to feel fearful will make you feel heightened enthusiasm instead,' she says.

Lastly, keep in mind a technique used in public speaking. Instead of thinking of butterflies in the stomach as nervousness, think of them as flying in formation, bringing you the adrenalin necessary to do an outstanding job!

Techniques for overcoming fear

1 To get over intimidation, put yourself in the situation six times and you will gain comfort.

2 When tense, tell your mind that you are relaxed, breathe deeply and drink water slowly.

3 When apprehensive, reframe the scenario in your mind, imagining yourself excited instead of apprehensive.

Do you try to show respect rather than arrogance?

'The first week in a new job is one of the eight most stressful experiences in life,' says trainer Phil Hawthorn. 'It's right up there in stress level with public speaking, divorce and moving house.' However, think about how you will handle your stress. How you let it show, or not show, will determine your level of professionalism.

Oliver Kelly remembers a new manager in his late twenties, who covered his insecurity by being very dismissive with staff and clients. 'I suppose arrogance is one way in which people cover up their fear when they are in a new position, but in the end it's detrimental to their success,' Oliver says. 'Instead, it's important to realize that no one expects you to know everything in a new job, and by asking questions and listening you will gain respect.'

Mary Kilgannon warns: 'It's natural to feel like a fish out of water when you start a new job, but don't cover up stress with arrogance. It's better to show respect for the way the company does things, and learn as you go. Remember that the people you'll be working with have more experience, and you can learn a lot from them.'

Do you reject back-stabbing?

One thing business owner Tomas Conefrey can't abide is back-stabbing from his staff. He handles it by going straight to them and explains that the job is hard enough without that. Even in challenging times he tells them, 'Look, I'm doing my best to keep you all in a job. I don't need any of this!' They get the message. It's important in management to set your boundaries with employees, and let those boundaries be known. Sometimes they forget that, if the business suffers, they might well be out of a job.

Some employers may not address the issue so directly, but they are aware of how it affects your work. They may even put people on probation without calling it that. More than one employer has said that they give people short-term assignments to see how they get on before offering them full-time work. They are watching behaviour and attitudes as much as working ability.

Business owner Evelyn Cochran talks about the importance of the first week in a job for new employees. 'I give new people a few hours of work at first, to see how it goes.' If they are hard working and pleasant, they get their hours extended. 'Being pleasant to other staff and customers is as important as being a good worker,' she says. 'If there's a problem, then it needs to be addressed with me or with other colleagues. Most problems can be resolved if there is good communication and understanding.'

Areas for improvement

After reading the above, which areas for improvement do you see applying to you? Is it being open to suggestions, or perhaps tackling intimidation head on? Is it self-control, or maybe changing your attitudes about authority? After reviewing the ten sections above, decide which ones you will tackle.

If you improve in all these ten attitudes, there'll be nothing to stop you from achieving the highest career results and promotion.

Summary

Today you had a chance to do a self-test on ten key attitudes. Some attitudes are better than others. Some get you promoted, others get you fired. It's better to discover which ones have room for improvement now than to discover them too late on the job. After all, you want to succeed in that job you've worked so hard to obtain.

Perhaps there were some qualities you hadn't considered before – such as being open to suggestions, considering yourself vital to the success of the company, or being willing to do what needs to be done – all of which will give your boss an impression of your promotability.

You've looked at your attitudes to authority, honesty, self-control, fear and intimidation and arrogance, and seen how management frowns on back-stabbing. Finally, you have had a chance to decide in which of these areas you need to take action, to bring you the highest career results.

SUNDAY
MONDAY
TUESDAY
WEDNESDAY
THURSDAY
FRIDAY
SATURDAY

Fact-check [answers at the back]

1. If your attitudes are not top-notch, at what level of your career will they hold you back the most?
   a) Senior management ❏
   b) Middle management ❏
   c) Entry level ❏
   d) All of the above ❏

2. Sticking to your old ways, no matter what your CEO, managing director or business owner suggests to you in the way of change, indicates what?
   a) That you are not open to suggestions and your job may be in jeopardy ❏
   b) That you are firm with your convictions and likely to be promoted ❏
   c) That you are quirky ❏
   d) None of the above ❏

3. If you want to succeed, is it important to have a 'willingness' attitude?
   a) Yes ❏
   b) No ❏
   c) Sometimes ❏
   d) It depends ❏

4. You can show that you are willing to train yourself by asking questions, but when is the best time to ask?
   a) All the time ❏
   b) When it's not disruptive ❏
   c) Whenever it strikes you to ask ❏
   d) Only when the other person invites you to ask ❏

5. If you have an issue with authority, how will you respond when your boss asks you to do something?
   a) You'll feel angry ❏
   b) You'll think you don't have time ❏
   c) You'll wonder 'why me?' ❏
   d) Any of the above ❏

6. What does lack of self-control on the job lead to?
   a) Mistrust ❏
   b) Inhibited job performance ❏
   c) Reduced promotion prospects ❏
   d) All of the above ❏

7. What's one way to overcome intimidation?
   a) Expose yourself to the situation repeatedly until a comfort level is reached ❏
   b) Go away and ponder it ❏
   c) Take your mind off it as soon as possible ❏
   d) None of the above ❏

8. If we let ourselves be fearful, which leads to narrowing of our arteries and restricted blood flow to the brain, what happens to our thinking?
   a) It gets faster ❏
   b) It's clearer ❏
   c) It's restricted ❏
   d) It's none of the above ❏

9. How do some people cover up their fear in a new position in a way that will be unpopular with colleagues?
a) Through truthfulness ❏
b) Through arrogance ❏
c) Through being tactful ❏
d) Through being polite ❏

10. Why do most bosses dislike seeing back-stabbing among their employees?
a) Because it creates a negative working environment ❏
b) Because it makes business suffer and can lead to you losing your job ❏
c) Because most problems can be solved when both sides listen and understand each other ❏
d) All of the above ❏

THURSDAY

When you're hired to lead

Whether you have been a manager before or not, it's worth learning some tricks of the trade that will make your journey more rewarding and successful.

As a leader, you'll want to consider potential resistance from the team in the beginning, and how to overcome it gracefully. You'll also want to consider the standards you'd like to maintain, and how to get everyone on board. You may have to deal with behaviour issues and you'll want to build loyalty. You'll want to consider change and how you'll lead that change effectively.

In this chapter we will look at:

- how to be effective when you are promoted from within
- what you'll need to learn when you are coming in from outside
- achieving leadership that soars
- how to achieve success when leading change.

When you're promoted from within

There are advantages and disadvantages to being promoted from within. According to trainer Phil Hawthorn, 70 per cent of people are promoted from within, so you're not alone if you face this situation. Others before you have succeeded, and so will you.

On the plus side, you'll know the company and the players. You'll have your own ideas about what needs to be done. You'll have conceptions of how well the people around you are doing their jobs, which may or may not prove to be true. You'll have better relationships with some of these people than others.

'It's best to mentally detach and take the attitude that you are new,' warns Maria MacMullan, a business analyst in the financial services industry. 'You are probably too familiar with some people, and not familiar enough with others. Be on your guard to make sure that you are communicating with everyone fairly.'

'There may well be resistance from some people,' she says. 'After all, you were their colleague one minute and now you are their boss.' In order to overcome that resistance, Maria recommends sitting down with each person on the team separately. 'Set up an appointment in advance and tell them that, since your position has changed, you want to touch base with them and get their input on things,' she advises.

You don't want to give them the impression, however, that they are being re-interviewed for their position. By saying you want their input, they won't feel threatened. Maria suggests that, over a cup of coffee, you say something like, 'I wanted to find out more about our team and how we can progress working together.' She says she thinks about each person in advance, and reviews her experience of working with them while keeping an open mind. In the meeting, she'll try to ascertain the person's strengths, interests and opinions.

When ending the meeting, she'll say, 'Look, we'll meet up again in a couple of weeks when I've found my feet, and we can strategize together.' This gives people the confidence that their opinions will be considered.

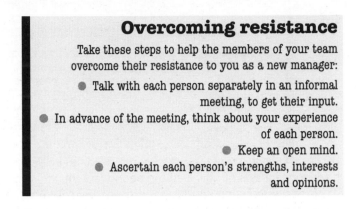

Overcoming resistance

Take these steps to help the members of your team overcome their resistance to you as a new manager:

● Talk with each person separately in an informal meeting, to get their input.
● In advance of the meeting, think about your experience of each person.
● Keep an open mind.
● Ascertain each person's strengths, interests and opinions.

Remember that the first few weeks can be difficult. People have their own agendas. But by sitting down and listening to them, you have a better chance of gaining their good opinion.

'In ending that first meeting with each person,' Maria says, 'I'll always say "I will link in with you and I will arrange another meeting. In the meantime, feel free to contact me if you need me." In that way you are sending the message that you are now in charge. You are no longer just colleagues.'

Keep in mind during these meetings that the following points are in your favour as the new boss:

● No one appreciates anything more than having their opinion heard.
● The team may have had to bottle up their ideas under the old boss, but now they have a chance for a fresh start with you.

Coming in from outside

When you come into management from outside, you have even more to learn. You'll be wondering what to expect from the team members, and they'll be wondering what to expect from you.

'You'll also benefit from having the same one-on-one conversations as mentioned above,' says Maria. You may discover some resistance, especially if your position was advertised internally, and people were turned down. But these one-on-one meetings will let people know that you respect them, and that their voices will be heard.

'Although you may not know the product or the processes, remember that you do understand the profession of management and you are the manager. You've proved yourself by getting the job,' says Maria. 'When you ask your staff questions that are product- and process-specific, you are acknowledging them while maintaining your authority as their manager.'

To maintain your authority while you settle in:

● ask questions that are product- and process-specific – this acknowledges people
● remember that you are the leader – you've proved it by being hired.

In the beginning, you'll be tempted to mentally compare the new environment to the old. That's a human trait. Nevertheless, Maria recommends keeping your opinions to yourself. 'Be wary of openly comparing the old place to your new place, either to employees or to upper management,' she says. 'This applies to both the good and the bad aspects of the job. In time you can change things, but for now you need to be impartial.'

Achieving leadership that soars

Maria recalls one manager, Joan, who stood out from the rest. 'She nurtured high performance by giving clear expectations and setting high standards,' she says. 'The others let things slide until they got out of hand. What I liked about Joan's management style,' says Maria, 'was that she maintained her professionalism at all times.'

Be clear on performance and deadlines

Joan would tell each individual and each group what was expected of them, in terms of the contents and deadlines of reports. 'Let's aim to have it finished sooner,' Joan would say, 'but next Friday is our absolute deadline.'

Then Joan would expect email updates from each person as the project went along. If she didn't receive those updates, she would ask the person or their supervisor. 'If anything stood in the way, if there was an IT problem or a person who couldn't be reached, she expected to hear about it and would help to resolve the issues so that the report met its deadline,' says Maria.

Halt failure in its tracks

Handling people who don't meet the mark is critical for success.

Here's how Joan handled it. First, she would circulate emails to the whole group, saying, 'Here are our goals. If you are not going to achieve the goal for any reason, let me know.' If a staff member was not making the target, she would ask a senior team member why. 'Is it a training problem or a lack of understanding?' she would ask.

Uphold standards

As a leader, it's important to set standards. These are standards that are important to you and the project. For each leader these can be different and it's important for you to establish your own.

'Joan would always come down hard if standards weren't met,' says Maria. "She would say things like, "This is not satisfactory. What we expect is xyz. I would have hoped this to be more fully analysed. Here's what we're going to do." Then she would lay out the timing and what needed to be done, even if it meant coming in early and staying late to get it finished,' says Maria.

Joan would often follow up her instructions by asking, 'Is this feasible?' In that way the employee would commit or not to the requested action, such as staying late until the project was completed correctly. If other projects were also in the pipeline, Joan might say, 'I'm aware that, by doing this, the other project might slip, but this is our priority.' Thus the employee knew exactly what the boss expected in terms of priorities.

Meeting standards and targets

To make sure that standards and targets are met, take the following steps:

1 Tell people what's not satisfactory, and what you expect instead.

2 Tell them what needs to be done to correct the situation.

3 Get buy-in with questions such as 'Is this feasible?'

4 Shift priorities if necessary to get the required results.

Tackle lack of integrity head on

What should you do if you discover a lack of integrity in a member of staff? This includes things like covering up, lateness, poor performance and attitude problems.

Maria recounts how Joan would retain her professionalism, even when discovering that an employee had lied about a piece of work. 'Other managers might ignore such behaviour and let it escalate to the point that other employees had to cover the work of their colleague,' Maria says. 'These managers might even talk about the offending employee behind their back, saying that the person couldn't be trusted.'

Joan, on the other hand, would tackle it head on, saying to the employee in question, 'Look, I've noticed such and such; is there anything "we" can be of assistance with to solve this problem?' By using the word 'we', she would be making the offending employee realize that the whole team was aware of and affected by their behaviour.

'Joan would always make an offending employee continue to do their own work. She never handed it on to another employee. She was highly respected by her staff for that,' says Maria.

> ## Handling integrity issues
>
> Here's what to do when you are faced with lack of integrity in a staff member:
>
> - Don't ignore the issue – it will only escalate and cause other concerns for you.
> - Handle problems quickly before they cause repercussions.
> - Tell the offender that you have noticed the situation and ask how 'we' can be of assistance.
> - Insist that the offender carry their load – never hand their work on to other people.

Leading change

Have you been brought in to make changes? Many of your staff members and colleagues will assume that you have, but if change doesn't happen in a timely fashion, they may get complacent and continue in their old ways. How long that window of opportunity remains open depends on several things: the urgency, the industry and the management team.

Pat Buckley is an organizational behaviour specialist. When discussing change, here are three things he likes asking individuals or groups:

1 What three things should we start doing?
2 What three things should we stop doing?
3 What does success look like to you?

Remember that personal success looks different to each person. When asking these questions, be prepared for surprises.

When Pat asked one company director what success looked like to him, here was his answer: 'Lying on a boat in the sunshine in the Mediterranean!' Pat then took the director through a series of steps, letting him decide what procedures he needed to put into place in order to run the business effectively from afar. 'Let's imagine that all is in order for you to be able to get away. What policies and procedures are needed, what personnel improvements are needed, who needs to be better trained, and who is capable of taking more responsibility?'

These same four questions work well for reaching any goal and assessing any organization:

● What policies and procedures are needed?
● What personnel improvements are needed?
● Who needs to be better trained?
● Who is capable of taking more responsibility?

When you need everyone on board

Once you've determined what needs changing, how do you get the support of the staff? Headhunter Adrian Evan's advice is to get all the appropriate data and necessary evidence for change. 'It's easier to get support when you have the statistics to prove that it needs to be done,' he says.

He remembers one key manager who handled it another way. Instead of going in with a mandate to the staff to cut a department, he solicited their input. 'Which departments need to be kept, and which need to go?' he asked them. After doing their analysis, the employees came up with the realizations themselves. This meant that there was less resentment and much more acceptance.

Getting to five-star performance

What if you're asked to dramatically raise the performance of existing personnel? Here's the story of how Dermot Fitzpatrick did it. His mandate was to take a three-star hotel to five stars, with existing staff members who were accustomed to operating in a three-star environment. His challenge was to train them to a new level – one they had never experienced – so he brought in experts from some of London's most prestigious hotels. 'I put together an A-team who served as mentors and trainers,' he says.

It is important for everyone involved to know the mission. His advice is this: 'Bring in everyone in order to explain the changes, including the outside suppliers.' In this case he told everyone – from staff to suppliers of bread, salmon, newspapers and transport – about the seamless service they now needed to provide. 'Our five-star service has to extend all the way out to the airport,' he told them.

Dermot trained his staff to cover for one another if they had to leave their post. 'Unfortunately, the day the inspector came in to judge our five-star worthiness, the porter had left his post unattended for a few short minutes,' he recounts. 'That meant another year of hard work to achieve the five stars.' He made his staff realize that people expect five-star service without interruption, and that no excuses will be tolerated.

Dermot now runs Inspiring Enterprises, serving as executive coach, facilitator and speaker to client companies that want exceptional growth and performance.

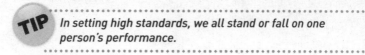

TIP *In setting high standards, we all stand or fall on one person's performance.*

When you need loyalty

It's important to be firm but fair, Dermot feels. 'You can't let one employee get away with something and then reprimand the next one for doing the same thing,' he says. At the same time, it's important to support people when they need it. 'If someone has a family problem, I would always circle the wagons to cover for them,' he says. That's the way loyalty is built.

When you need behaviour to change

Sometimes employees need to be given guidelines for their behaviour. Simon Stevens remembers a staff member who wanted things done on her own terms. 'Once I was busy preparing a report with a deadline and Sally came up to me, demanding some information. I explained that I would get it for her in a moment, and that the report was not due until later, but she continued to ask me numerous times.' The way Simon handled it was to talk to the employee directly about her behaviour: 'Here's what I experienced today. You did xyz. In future I'd like you to respect my time too.' The incident never repeated itself.

> ## Handling behaviour issues
>
> Here are some steps to take when you are faced with a behaviour issue:
>
> 1 Talk with the person involved in private.
> 2 Tell them what you experienced.
> 3 State what they did, succinctly.
> 4 Tell them what you would like done differently in the future; be specific.

Summary

Being hired to lead is an honour and a privilege, whether you're promoted from within or hired from outside. Today you learned that, despite the possibility of finding some early resistance from the team, especially from the people who wanted your job, by asking the right questions you can put people at ease while still establishing your authority.

To achieve a 'leadership that soars', you saw the importance of being clear on performance expectations and deadlines. You saw how to stop failure in its tracks, how to uphold standards and how to tackle lack of integrity head on.

In leading change, you learned what questions to ask that will help you assess what changes need to be made and how to engage the team in reaching the required results, while building loyalty. You also learned about resolving behaviour issues through an effective statement process.

SUNDAY MONDAY TUESDAY WEDNESDAY THURSDAY FRIDAY SATURDAY

Fact-check [answers at the back]

1. To overcome resistance and get people on your side when you're promoted, what should you do?
   a) Talk with each person and get their input ❏
   b) Keep an open mind ❏
   c) Ascertain each person's strengths, interests and opinions ❏
   d) All of the above ❏

2. How should you establish your authority early on?
   a) Lead daily staff meetings ❏
   b) Tell each person about your experience ❏
   c) After meeting one-on-one, set a follow-up meeting and tell them that in the meantime they can contact you if they need you ❏
   d) After meeting one-on-one, offer to go out for a drink together ❏

3. When coming in from outside, how can you succeed with people who had hoped to land your job themselves?
   a) Find out what they see themselves doing ❏
   b) Ask what they see can be done in certain areas ❏
   c) Be understanding ❏
   d) All of the above ❏

4. How important is it to give clear instructions on performance expectations and deadlines?
   a) It's not important ❏
   b) It's essential ❏
   c) It's awkward, so you should avoid it ❏
   d) It's best not to do it – it's micro-managing ❏

5. When a person is failing to meet the required performance, what do you need to find out?
   a) Whether it's a training problem or a lack of understanding ❏
   b) What other people think of them ❏
   c) How soon you can get rid of them ❏
   d) Who can take over some of their work ❏

6. When you find lack of integrity, such as lying or attitude problems, what's the best way to handle it?
   a) Disregard it ❏
   b) Talk to the offender, state the problem and ask how you can assist ❏
   c) Discuss it with others when the person is not around ❏
   d) Take comfort in knowing you don't have the same problem ❏

7. When you are trying to assess what changes need to be made, what questions should you ask?

a) What three things should we start doing? ❏

b) What three things should we stop doing? ❏

c) What does success look like to you? ❏

d) All of the above ❏

8. Once you've determined the changes that need to be made, what's a good way to get staff support for those changes?

a) Give data and evidence proving the necessity of the action ❏

b) Give examples of how other firms do it successfully ❏

c) State the goal and engage the staff in the analysis leading to the decision ❏

d) All of the above ❏

9. In setting high standards, how can you start to raise the performance of existing personnel?

a) Make sure everyone involved knows the mission ❏

b) Warn them that under-performance will not be tolerated ❏

c) Promise them a bonus if they succeed ❏

d) Tell them you're hoping for the best ❏

10. It's important to be firm but fair, according to one manager. What did he mean?

a) Give each person the same tongue lashing publicly ❏

b) Give each person the same pay increase, or no increase ❏

c) Give recognition ❏

d) You can't let one person do something and then reprimand the next for doing the same thing ❏

FRIDAY

Leadership dos and don'ts

Good leadership starts with making sure that everyone knows what's expected. People also want to discover how they can best use their skills and talents, so your role involves engaging people and giving them the right level of challenge.

Leadership means supporting your team members when they need it most, thus gaining their loyalty. It involves communicating up and down the line, and doing all that you commit to do. It involves giving recognition where recognition is due, and handling difficulties skilfully and on the spot.

Today you will learn these seven essential leadership rules:

1 Show what's expected and engage creativity.
2 Give responsibility and challenges.
3 Give support to gain loyalty.
4 Communicate up and down the line.
5 Don't rely on memory.
6 Give recognition.
7 Handle difficult situations head on.

Show what's expected and engage creativity

In my career as a trainer and speaker, I have the opportunity to meet hundreds of managers. Some stand out as exceptional. David Pearson was one of those. We met when Sony hired me as keynote speaker for their annual conference.

David was brought in by Sony to head a UK consumer products division, and his mandate was to take sales from £150 million to £250 million in three years. It was a tall order. He remembers his first Japanese boss, who explained the culture of the company and what he expected from David.

The boss started by drawing a circle with a horizontal line through it. On the upper half he wrote the name of the company, and all it represented – such as policies, brands and values. On the lower half he wrote David's name, and all it represented – such as his skills, experience, values and creativity.

The boss explained how he saw the merging of the two. 'I want you to follow company policy,' the boss told him, 'but I also want you to bring in your own skills, talents and creativity.' This synergy would be the key to success.

'I found that to be very empowering,' says David. 'It allowed me to be creative in bringing the best out of people to reach our goals.' The team did just that under David's leadership; in fact, they exceeded the goal by £50 million. David now acts as Chair and non-executive director for other companies, bringing the skills he acquired to the table. In his book, *The 20 Ps of Marketing*, he shows how every company's ability to harness creativity is essential to its success.

Leading your team

Think now of the team you will lead.

- What can you do to show them what's expected?
- How can you engage their creativity in order to reach your goals?

Jot down your ideas now, while they are fresh in your mind.

Give responsibility and challenges

If you're privileged to lead, it's important to think about how you will keep people motivated. Giving them responsibilities and challenges is usually an effective method.

Like many talented people, Aisling Brady wants to be given extra responsibility and the opportunity to do more. 'This prevents boredom on the job,' she says. 'It makes people grow. Even when you make a mistake, it gives you the opportunity to improve and come back to do even better next time.'

Paul Murray puts it another way: 'Challenges inspire people and give them confidence,' he says. 'I like to report to managers who are willing to throw me in at the deep end.' In his first week with a venture capital company, he was able to mentor a start-up company using his electronic engineering expertise. 'I enjoy not knowing what's coming up, and doing things I've not done before. It's a great feeling and it gives me a sense that they trust me,' he says.

Even volunteers are motivated in the same way. Claire Ayres volunteers for the National Trust, and she points to her head of department as an excellent example of good leadership.

'Much of our time is spent scanning photographs and archiving them, which he knows can be monotonous,' she says. 'Therefore he asks us to think of creative ways to use the photographs as we're scanning them. That makes the time fly by, and has led to creative projects, including the merging of 1930s interviews and photographs, making highly interesting historical presentations.'

What Claire's boss has done is to look at the work from the staff's point of view, and then think of ways to get a creative outcome. As some would say, he knows how to turn lemons into lemonade!

> ## Challenging your team
>
> Think now of the people in your own team.
> - What can you do to give them more responsibility?
> - How can you offer them interesting challenges?
>
> Jot down your ideas now.

Give support to gain loyalty

Seamus Gill is a civil servant who remembers one exceptional manager, whose actions inspired loyalty. Seamus was in a situation where he was overloaded with work due to a staff shortage. He found himself with more cases to cover than he could handle in the time allocated.

He talked with his boss about it, and he was surprised when the boss offered to take one file off his load and handle it himself, instead of reallocating it to another employee. Seamus never forgot how he had been helped out at a stressful time.

Two years later, the boss called him, asking for his help on a project. He said, 'Seamus, you are perfectly entitled to say no. But you would really be helping me out if you could assist me. If you say no, I'll think none the worse of you.' Seamus didn't hesitate. He agreed to return the favour of two years earlier and assist instantly, remembering the boss's supportiveness of him when he needed it.

TIP *If we want to engender support and loyalty, we need to lead by example.*

SUNDAY
MONDAY
TUESDAY
WEDNESDAY
THURSDAY
FRIDAY
SATURDAY

Communicate up and down the line

'It's important, in a fast-growing environment, to communicate up and down the line,' says Louise Richardson, head of HR and training for a UK childcare company that's grown from 10 to 180 staff in only three years. 'It's also important to act as a role model for communication for those with less experience,' she says.

In her industry it's important to keep everyone informed and working in line with the education authority. 'Therefore I find it useful to run issues past my boss, before going to speak to staff members,' she says. That way, everyone is informed consistently.

As for one-to-one communication, it helps to repeat what you've heard. What managing director Elizabeth Carter appreciated was the way her assistant would double-check to make sure that communication was correct. After being given the assignment, Sharon would repeat it back: 'So you want me to redo this section and then get it back to you. Is that right?' This method of double-checking avoids many problems and a good deal of frustration.

In fact, I use the repeat method to summarize what's been agreed in meetings. For example, I might say, 'So what we've all agreed is this. John, you'll have the report done by Wednesday. Mary, you'll talk to David by Wednesday, and we'll conference call on Thursday. Are we all agreed?'

Mastering communication

Laurie Erskine remembers the best manager she ever had in the US. 'It was with Disney Cruise Lines,' she says, 'and our boss had an amazing handle on everything. She knew what she wanted, how to motivate, and how to manage everything with humour. You could tell she loved her job overseeing 50 people.

'She communicated throughout the organization – with the cruise line, the port authority, the managers under her, and the employees,' says Laurie. 'She led morning meetings with all managers and staff twice a week. In a 20-minute briefing, she would mention any celebrities coming on board, and any issues with immigration and customs. We were always aware of all the issues that might affect us.'

'When we were helping passengers check in, the immediate supervisors took care of everything, but she would come along occasionally to check on things,' says Laurie. 'She was very hands-on and always available. She was obviously the number one authority – everyone supported whatever she decided. She was such a good communicator and always had a positive attitude.'

What about communicating potential problems? Brenda Smyth likes to 'manage the small things, so that big things don't arise.' When she sees a potential problem cropping up, she communicates it to her seniors. 'Just to let you know, xyz happened.' This allows senior managers to be aware and act accordingly if they see fit.

She also believes that, if an employee needs guidance, it's important to give it. For example, if she sees that an employee isn't capturing enough information in writing, she might say to them, 'Would you mind taking down more detail in the client meetings?'

'Manage the small things, so that bigger problems don't arise.'

Communicating with excellence

Think now of your own organization.

- What can you do to excel in communication up and down the line?
- How can you excel in one-to-one communication?

Jot down your ideas now.

Don't rely on memory

How far will you get in life if you rely on memory to honour your commitments or remember important facts from meetings? Not far, because the human mind forgets 60 per cent of what it hears within hours.

I remember an incident that happened in London when I was Chair of the Chamber of Commerce. It was a Wednesday and we had just finished a meeting of the Board of Directors. Late that afternoon, I was walking down Oxford Street when I bumped into William, one of our board members. 'Oh, hi, William,' I said. 'By the way, when will you be able to get back to the Board with the information you promised?'

I was stunned when I heard his reply: 'What information is that?' he asked. It had only been three hours since the meeting, and he had already forgotten his commitment. William, although an executive, had not yet learned this important point.

TIP *Research shows that everyone forgets 60 per cent of what they've heard after a few hours. What's the answer? Notes, of course. It's the solution, regardless of your position.*

An additional way to handle commitments is to take action immediately. One of the best executives I've had the privilege to know always carries his mobile phone and actions most of his commitments on the spot. While talking to me at an event, he called his office and said, 'Can you please get that report over to Christine's office? Thanks.' Done. His mind no longer needed to carry it, and I knew it was done.

Capturing information

Think now of your own working life.

● What can you do to make sure you capture important information?

● What can you do to ensure that you honour your commitments?

Jot down your ideas now.

Give recognition

Pippa Lee of Lifecollege.org now takes the good management she's experienced from her past into her own training company. 'One of the great managers I had was excellent at motivating,' she says. 'He used to bring us together twice a year for product announcements and awards, such as highest sales and other achievements.' There were bottles of wine as prizes, plus bonuses. 'But, above all, it was the recognition that meant the most to us,' says Pippa.

Effective recognition doesn't need to involve monetary rewards. Now, in her training company, Pippa tries to recognize the skills and natural attributes of her trainers. 'We were setting up the training room one day and one of my trainers, who is particularly good at detail, noticed that the blinds were askew,' says Pippa. 'When she went over to fix them, I thanked her for it.' The trainer was surprised and said, 'Well, thanks – some people say I'm being obsessive, so thanks for recognizing it as a strength.'

Thus recognition leads to loyalty and heightened performance. In fact, recognition has so many uses that I encourage all aspiring leaders to become experts in it. If you wish to know more, you can read about seven ways to heighten performance and productivity in my book *People Skills In A Week*.

One method you'll read about is called the Dolphin Method. In using that method, you choose a performance or productivity level you want an employee to reach, and then reinforce the steps to getting there. It's a bit like the way dolphins are trained to reach higher and higher jump levels, by providing positive reinforcement at each step of the way.

The military organizations of the world have an excellent tradition of giving recognition through plaques, medals and presentations. This custom instils gratitude, loyalty and higher performance. Here's part of the wording my son received in his achievement metal for civilian service: 'During the period of ... Mr Thomas Harvey distinguished himself by producing exceptional results in ... His performance reflects great credit upon himself, the NATO Support Activity, The Brussels Community and The United States Army.' This kind of recognition can be created for all levels in any industry. Why not do it for your team members?

People deserve recognition for what they do. Recognition works in business, in the community, in personal relationships, and in the family. Why not set out to master it now? Your future success may depend on it.

Handle difficult situations head on

'When things go wrong with staff members, put yourself in their place before you get upset,' says manager and chemist John Miles. 'Step back and ask yourself, "Would I have done any better?"' However, it's also important to give a good roasting when needed, but you have to do it in an encouraging way. For example, John might say, 'You let yourself down; you can do better!'

I really like John's way of putting that. Rather than leaving the employee with a negative feeling, it leaves them with a higher level of aspiration for themselves and with the feeling that the boss has faith in them.

When dealing with a difficult situation, always use methods that leave employees feeling they can do better and that you have faith in them.

Oliver Kelly recalls one manager who had a weak member of staff and, rather than addressing the weaknesses, he let the matter slide. 'Eventually, client issues arose and business was lost. Then upper management had to get involved, and the manager looked bad.' If the manager had handled the problem as soon as it arose, his career would have been saved and so would the client.

What if you are asked to do something that you suspect is illegal or immoral? Attorney Martin Hughes advises employees to write everything down and date it. This allows you to sit back and assess the situation away from the heat of the moment. On reflection, things may be different from the way they first appear. The last thing you want to do is to make a false accusation. But if your suspicions prove to be true, you at least have documentation of statements and dates if you need it in court.

Paul Murray, in venture capital, has a lot of people coming in for funding and most often his company has to say no. That's difficult, but Paul looks at it this way. 'When giving bad news, whether it's in venture capital, a job appraisal or something else, there is a good way and a bad way to do it. The wrong way leaves the individual feeling negative or hopeless. The right way leaves them feeling uplifted and positive.'

Handling difficult situations

Think now of some difficult situations *you* might face.

● How would you handle a problem with a staff member?
● How would you deal with being asked to do something illegal or immoral?
● How would you give bad news to someone in your team?

Jot down your ideas now.

Summary

Today we looked at seven areas of leadership dos and don'ts. We saw that good leaderships starts with making sure that everyone knows what's expected of them as well as how they can use their skill and creativity to meet the goals.

We discussed the importance of giving responsibility and challenges, as well as support when it's most needed. This will build loyalty and enhance performance.

There were examples of communicating up and down the line, as well as the importance of not relying on your memory, since 60 per cent of what we hear is forgotten within hours. The use of notes and taking immediate action will get you known for reliability and therefore recognized as suitable for promotion.

Giving recognition, we learned, leads to higher performance and productivity. In handling difficult situations it's important to tackle them head on, using methods that leave employees feeling that they can do better and that you have faith in them.

SUNDAY

MONDAY

TUESDAY

WEDNESDAY

THURSDAY

FRIDAY

SATURDAY

Fact-check [answers at the back]

1. What is one of the greatest things a boss can do for managers?
   a) Empower them to use their creativity in reaching their goals ❑
   b) Not micro-manage ❑
   c) Empower them to set their own goals ❑
   d) Not require feedback ❑

2. What does giving people responsibility and challenges achieve?
   a) It prevents boredom on the job ❑
   b) It makes people grow ❑
   c) It gives people the opportunity to improve and do a better job next time ❑
   d) All of the above ❑

3. What's a good way to gain loyalty from staff?
   a) Let staff handle things their own way, even if it conflicts with company policy ❑
   b) Give them support when they need it ❑
   c) Don't have any set hours ❑
   d) None of the above ❑

4. When given an assignment, what's a good way to make sure that you have understood your boss's intent?
   a) Move ahead based on past experience ❑
   b) Ask a colleague ❑
   c) Repeat what you heard the boss say ❑
   d) Start the project and check in with the boss at the midway point ❑

5. If an employee is clearly not doing the job well, what should you do?
   a) Wait until they change departments and let the next boss handle it ❑
   b) Correct them in front of their peers to teach everyone a lesson at once ❑
   c) Ask a more senior person to handle it ❑
   d) Assume they need guidance and coach them on the correct way to do it ❑

6. Will a good manager always make staff aware of anything that might affect them?
   a) Yes ❑
   b) No ❑
   c) Sometimes ❑
   d) It's not important ❑

7. Humans forget 60 per cent of what they hear within a few hours, so what is the purpose of keeping notes of important points?
   a) To increase effectiveness ❑
   b) To keep our commitments ❑
   c) To be responsible ❑
   d) All of the above ❑

8. What can giving recognition for a job well done help your staff achieve?
   a) Higher performance ❑
   b) A bonus ❑
   c) Notoriety ❑
   d) A false sense of confidence ❑

9. If you sense some serious wrongdoings are aimed at you, what's one way to handle the situation?
a) Write down the incidents and date them ❏
b) Realize that you may need documentation if a case goes to court ❏
c) Sit back and assess the situation away from the heat of the moment ❏
d) All of the above ❏

10. When giving out bad news, there is a wrong way and a right way to do it. What does the right way leave a person feeling?
a) Angry but determined ❏
b) Uplifted and positive ❏
c) Foolish but committed ❏
d) In awe of you as their manager ❏

SATURDAY

Reaching your goals

You've had a full week in the new job. You've met your boss and colleagues, you know your targets and you know what's expected of you. Now it's time to segment your targets and decide how you'll monitor them to achieve success.

You'll need to set your first priority connected with your goal and hit the ground running. You'll have to discover the 'why' when things go wrong. You may have to train others and then monitor their success.

At times, your success will depend on other people, even when they don't report to you. How will you get their co-operation? How will you head off their failure to deliver, especially when they don't manage their time well? When all else fails, how will you use the resources of management to make sure you achieve the results you want?

All these questions will be answered today, as well as other questions you can use to monitor and achieve success. You will learn how to:

- set targets for your success
- train and monitor for success
- deal with others when *your* success relies on them.

Set targets for your success

When Janet Lim from Singapore decided to leave the jewellery business for car sales, she knew her starting salary would only be *one-fifth* of what she had been making, but the potential of the new job was huge. She knew she would have to motivate herself to learn new products, find out about customers and discover the culture of the company. After some soul searching, she decided what her top three motivators would be. With these, she managed to grow her salary to five times that of a college graduate, despite not having a degree, and to be featured in my book *Secrets of the World's Top Sales Performers*.

These were her motivators:

1 Enjoy the industry.
2 Use curiosity to learn.
3 Have financial desire.

What are your motivators?

Think about your job now.

● Now that you've been there a week, what do you think you'll like most?
● What will you enjoy learning?
● What will motivate you to succeed?

Make a list of your own top three motivators.

When Philip Drucker was trying to decide whether he should accept an offer with a major financial services company, he knew he would have to double the size of the operations in two years in order to achieve his personal and financial goals. That would mean recruiting new staff members and retaining others. It would mean examining the existing operation to see how to maximize its potential. It was a tall order.

In two years, Philip not only achieved his goal but he also managed to attain the second-highest revenue growth of all the company's branches in the US.

Let's look at what he did. 'Taking the leap to the new job wasn't easy,' says Philip. 'The biggest hurdle was embracing the challenge to meet those targets.' He remembers the advice he had from a person who had hired him 20 years earlier: 'To be successful, you have to move out of your comfort zone.' In his case, that meant leaving behind a branch he had built up over many years.

Staying would have been the easy route. But without challenges, we don't grow. Life becomes mundane and repetitive. If we want to keep our spirit alive, we need to take the challenging path.

'To be successful, you have to move out of your comfort zone.'

On reflection, Philip isn't sure he would have been able to achieve the goal in the new company if there had not been a lot riding on it. To put it another way, he says: 'The consequences of *not* succeeding are very motivating!' In his previous position, he had taken the operation from $6 million to $20 million. In this one he would have to do the same in half the time. 'I had to hit the ground running,' says Philip.

SUNDAY

MONDAY

TUESDAY

WEDNESDAY

THURSDAY

FRIDAY

SATURDAY

The first priority

Recruitment was his first priority. 'It helps to be in the marketplace for 18 years and be known,' he says. He wanted good people from the industry, and had tried to recruit some of them before. 'Of course, they want to know why you are changing companies, so that they can assess the potential for themselves. The opportunities in the new company were appealing.' After joining the company, it took him only two months to recruit the new people.

The second priority

'Retention was ultimately important too,' he says. 'I knew I was inheriting a good team, and success depended on keeping them.' Between recruitment efforts, he focused on getting to know his team, their strengths, ideas and strategies – that meant a lot of dinners and lunches. Eventually, 60 per cent of his team would be made up of his retained advisers.

Obviously, Philip made clear targets for himself. Let's look at how he monitors and controls activity to stay on course.

'We can do a lot of tracking of who does what compared to last year,' he says. 'If someone is not performing, I need to find out why. Did his or her biggest client leave? If so, what are they going to do to replace that?'

'I've always been a numbers guy,' he says. He asks questions to discover the strengths and areas of potential growth of his advisers. 'Tell me about your clients; do you have a relationship with the next generation?' he might ask.

Figure out the 'why'

When looking for problems or growth opportunities in your team, he advises managers as follows. 'Figure out the "why". Then be prescriptive.' He remembers a team that had worked well in the past, but over time the dynamics changed. When asked who did what, their answer was: 'Oh, we all do it.' Once they realized that there were too many grey areas of responsibility, they divided into smaller units for higher accountability and productivity. The grey areas answered 'why' their results had changed.

He's also not afraid to tell people if they need to improve. 'Experience is knowing a mistake before it happens,' he says.

Let the results be known

As for targets and accountability, Philip advises managers to let individual results be known. 'Anything you measure will bring results,' he says. 'If you have 20 people, you might publish results for the top four or five achievers in different categories,' he says. 'But you don't need to announce who is dead last – they'll figure that out themselves.'

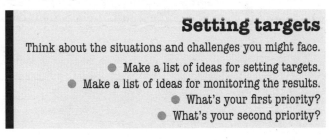

Setting targets

Think about the situations and challenges you might face.

● Make a list of ideas for setting targets.
● Make a list of ideas for monitoring the results.
● What's your first priority?
● What's your second priority?

Train and monitor for success

Bill Laswick, who owns the Laswick Insurance Agency, provides the highest level of service I've ever experienced in the US or Europe. His staff are remarkably well trained, reliable and efficient. On top of that, they're personable and a pleasure to work with. I asked him how he manages to train and monitor for that level of success.

'If people are right for the job, I can tell within a week,' says Bill. Here's how he finds out:

● When someone is hired, he tells them what's expected.
● He trains them to keep a list of who called in, and what was promised. If they promised to call back with a quote by the end of the day, then this must be carried out on time.
● In the beginning, he'll sit with them each morning and ask, 'Did you make these calls?' or 'Did you follow up with those people?'

Review as required

In the beginning he reviews their work daily for a certain period, then weekly and then monthly. He adds new responsibilities on a regular basis. 'Initially, it's a lot of work, but it's worth it,' he says.

'In my industry, it's all about having the right people. They need an inner drive to get things right, not just do what's necessary to get by. They need to be perfectionists and they need to enjoy delivering *more* than they promise.'

'Some people can multi-task, but others can't. You can teach people technology, but if they can't handle pressure, then they're in the wrong business,' he says. 'When you choose the right people to work with, you have less to monitor. You won't be afraid to answer the phone or afraid of having problems to face, because all is in order.'

'It's essential to have support around you,' says Bill. 'Attitude is everything. If it's 5 p.m., are they going to go home or wait for the client who calls to say they are dropping off a policy? The whole quality of life changes when you have the right people and they're trained,' he says.

Think of your situation now. If you have staff members, who needs to be trained? What will that mean to your quality of life? What do you need to monitor and review in their activities, and how often? What can be added to their responsibilities? As Bill said, it's a lot of work in the beginning, but the results are worth it.

Reviewing, monitoring and training

Think about your employees.

- What are their responsibilities?
- What can you add to their responsibilities?
- What needs monitoring and reviewing?
- What are your training goals?

Jot down your ideas now.

When your success relies on others

Often your success will rely on the co-operation of others. How do you handle getting support from another department, for example? A lot depends on the protocol in your organization. Perhaps your boss will contact the other department to let them know you need their support.

'After that, I like to go straight to the person involved,' says Darrin Braddy, project lead in an engineering company. 'By sitting down face to face, I'm able to explain exactly what is needed and agree on deadlines.'

Darrin makes a good point. If you rely on delivering a message through your boss, to another and then another, your communication becomes diluted. 'I often find that I can get the information or decision I need at that first meeting,' she says, 'whereas trying to do it through layers of other people leads to mountains of miscommunication and delay.'

This point, about face-to-face effectiveness, reminds me of a highly respected woman from Tokyo, whom I quoted in my book *In Pursuit of Profit*. She has been adviser to not one but *four* prime ministers. Her advice about communication is this: 'Never write when you can call, and never call when you can visit.' The next time you need something important, consider a quick visit instead of an email. You'll be amazed at the results.

> **'Never write when you can call, and never call when you can visit.'**

Head off failure to deliver

Let's look at what's next. You've communicated what you need and you've agreed on when it will be delivered. But what if people don't follow through?

'It's a little tricky when you're not their boss and your results rely on their information or actions,' says Darrin. She usually heads it off in that first meeting by saying, for example, 'OK, John, that's great – I'll look forward to getting that information from you as we agreed next Friday, and I'll just check in with you on Tuesday to make sure everything is on track. Is that all right with you?'

In this way, you are making sure that people are committing to what's been agreed. Secondly, you're making it clear that you intend to monitor their actions, which heightens the chance that they will follow through.

'The good people will jump on your request right away,' says Darrin. 'They want to get it off their plate.' She reckons that about a quarter of the people she deals with fall into that category. 'The other 75 per cent may be busy, forget or not care, which is why it's important to check in with them before your drop-dead date,' she says.

When people can't manage their time

When calling people or emailing to check on their progress, you might say, 'Hi John, how is that project coming along?' If the colleague then indicates that there might be problems meeting the deadline, Darrin suggests saying, 'Is there a time you can set aside and dedicate to it over the next two days?' She's found this to be effective with people who have trouble managing their time. 'By asking them that specific question, you are putting the idea into their mind of when they can do it,' she says.

On the personal side of communication, she has two pieces of advice. First, be highly professional. 'Always be very nice, polite, helpful and cheerful. Secondly, when you finish your conversation, don't linger. Leave or hang up. This lets them know that you value your time and theirs too,' she says. 'You're more likely to get a positive result from them than if they think it's a casual visit,' she advises.

TIP *Keep your attitude to colleagues friendly and cheerful but always professional.*

When all else fails

What if, despite the fact that you have monitored the progress of a piece of work, you discover that you're not going to meet the deadline due to the lack of the promised information or support? The important thing to remember is that *you* are the one who is 100-per-cent responsible. This includes meeting the deadline, regardless of the encumbrances. Excuses don't work. It's essential to go all out to get what's needed, and keep your boss informed when hurdles crop up.

'It's frustrating,' says Darrin, 'but you can always go to your manager. Perhaps he or she can speak with the other manager. Or they can bring in resources, authorize extra hours or buy new software – whatever is needed to meet the target,' she says.

Reaching your targets

Think about the interdepartmental and other issues that might crop up when you need to rely on others to reach your targets.

- How will you gain the support and co-operation of others?
- How will you maintain good communication?
- How will you make sure that they deliver what they promised?
- How will you check progress?

Make a note of some of the techniques you might use to help you guarantee success.

Summary

When taking on a new challenge, be it a project, a department or an organization, we need to face the hurdles head on. This means getting out of our comfort zone and setting specific targets and deadlines to make sure we succeed. The new targets motivate us because everything rides on achieving them.

Usually, we have to hit the ground running. We have to set our first priority and our second. We have to stay focused, monitor our results, and teach our teams to do the same. We have to look for problems and growth opportunities and figure out the 'why' before determining action.

When we need support or information from people outside our direct influence, it's important to get commitment to deadlines and then monitor progress. If people can't manage their time, we can help by asking the right questions. We can also ask management to bring in extra resources.

The important thing to remember is that we are 100-per-cent responsible for our success or failure, regardless of difficulties.

Fact-check [answers at the back]

1. In order to accept new challenges, what do we have to be willing to do?
   a) Have resources set aside ❏
   b) Get out of our comfort zone ❏
   c) Get the support of family ❏
   d) None of the above ❏

2. When setting high targets for yourself, what should you determine?
   a) Exactly what you need to achieve and when ❏
   b) Your first priority ❏
   c) Your second priority ❏
   d) All of the above ❏

3. When managing people who aren't performing as they should, what should you not be afraid to do?
   a) Offend them ❏
   b) Shout ❏
   c) Embarrass them ❏
   d) Tell them they need to improve ❏

4. Before deciding how to solve a problem, what should you find out?
   a) The 'why' ❏
   b) The 'where' ❏
   c) The 'when' ❏
   d) All of the above ❏

5. Why should you let results be known?
   a) To motivate staff ❏
   b) To show people who's boss ❏
   c) It's not important ❏
   d) It's good for the boss ❏

6. In providing the highest level of service, what do people need to do?
   a) Deliver just what's promised ❏
   b) Do what's necessary to get by ❏
   c) Have an inner drive to get things right ❏
   d) All of the above ❏

7. What will you have when you choose the right people to work with?
   a) More to monitor ❏
   b) Less to monitor ❏
   c) The same to monitor ❏
   d) None of the above ❏

8. What should you do when someone promises you information that you need in order to do your work?
   a) Get their agreement on their delivery date ❏
   b) Get their commitment to their delivery date ❏
   c) Check in midway to see how it's going ❏
   d) All of the above ❏

9. When people can't manage their time, what's one way to handle it?
   a) Call and check on their progress ❏
   b) Ask them if there is a time they can set aside to do it ❏
   c) Ask questions that give them ideas of when they can do it ❏
   d) Any of the above ❏

10. If all else fails and you can't get what you need, what can you talk to your boss about?

a) Speaking to the other manager ☐
b) Bringing in resources ☐
c) Doing whatever is necessary ☐
d) Any of the above ☐

7 × 7

1 Seven keys to success

- Determine the strengths you bring to the job, and focus on how they fit the needs of your company.
- Set your priorities and goals early on. Stay focused and be prepared to hit the ground running.
- Establish your credibility by mastering the way you speak about yourself and your experience.
- Ask whether there is a review process and, if so, what's included in it.
- When you see changes that need to be made, tell your boss how those changes will help the organization. Sell your concepts by pointing out the benefits of your ideas.
- Master the ten attitudes that can get you promoted. Be open to suggestions, consider yourself vital to the company's success, stay motivated, train yourself, have a positive attitude towards authority, use integrity, have self-control, handle fear and insecurity, and reject back-stabbing.
- When you are hired to lead, be clear on performance expectations and deadlines.

2 Seven things to avoid

- Don't leave your results to chance. Ninety per cent of people who write their goals down achieve them.
- Don't waste time and effort doing something different from what's expected. Clarify your project or assignment before you begin.
- Don't rely on memory. Record your commitments, assignments and deadlines.

- If you're in management, don't be afraid to give more responsibility, and let employees know you have confidence in them.
- Don't ignore the gaps in your CV. Find ways in this job, or in a membership association, to gain the missing experience.
- Don't let problems fester. If your boss is taking credit for your work, say: 'Boss, I'd like a piece of the credit.' If your employee is underperforming, say: 'You let yourself down; you can do better.'
- Don't ignore targets. Break them down into daily, weekly and monthly activities. Then implement them, and monitor your results against those targets

3 Seven ways to motivate

- Verbalize your satisfaction in working with people: 'John, I enjoyed working with you on the project.' Everyone needs a boost.
- Since 60 per cent of a person's self-image is related to their job, point out the strengths you see in people. It will create job satisfaction and raise morale.
- Everyone needs support and motivation – even your boss. Ask questions about their area of interest and listen intently to their answers. Few people do, so you will stand out.
- Use positive vocabulary and an enthusiastic attitude. That will have a magnetic effect rather than a repelling effect caused by negativity.
- Tell your boss, colleagues and employees what you appreciate about them: 'Boss, I really appreciated your positive feedback on that project' or, 'Sam, I appreciate that I can rely on your punctuality.'
- Take personal responsibility for good communication. Each person is different, so you'll need to use different styles to be effective.
- Consider yourself to be a motivator of others. When you do, your career and personal satisfaction will skyrocket.

4 Seven ways to get the job done

- Be clear about the objective. Say: 'Boss, let me feed back to you what I understand about this project, to make sure we're on the same track. I don't want to waste your time or mine.'
- Be clear about deadlines. Say: 'Mary, I understand this needs to go to corporate on Friday. Is that your understanding?'
- If you are relying on work from others, call them a few days ahead of the deadline to see how they are doing. Take corrective action if necessary.
- If you see problems cropping up, tackle them early on. Don't wait until it is too late to correct. Say: 'Boss, I'm not sure we need to worry about this yet, but I thought we might discuss it so that I can get your thoughts.'
- There are always grey areas of responsibility. Don't be afraid to step up and do the job if it's necessary to meet the deadline or objective.
- Don't be afraid to defend yourself if you are right. Say: 'Yes boss, I did send that email because I had approval from Joe who oversees the project.'
- Keep your boss up to date with quick status reports. This will allow them to make interim adjustments if things go off course. They can also use the information to keep others up to date and look good themselves.

5 Seven great quotes

- 'In the end, it's not the years in your life that count. It is the life in your years.' Abraham Lincoln (1809–65), President of the United States, lawyer and American civil war leader preserving the US as one nation
- 'Strong minds discuss ideas, average minds discuss events, weak minds discuss people.' Socrates (470–399 BCE), Greek philosopher
- 'Anger is never without a reason, but seldom with a good one.' Benjamin Franklin (1706–90), American statesman, scientist and author

- 'Success is not final. Final is not fatal: it is the courage to continue that counts.' Winston Churchill (1874–1965), British Prime Minister, wartime leader, historian and writer
- 'Fear is incomplete knowledge.' Agatha Christie (1890–1976), British author and playwright
- 'Opportunities don't often come along. So when they do, you have to grab them.' Audrey Hepburn (1929–93), British Academy Award winning actress and humanitarian, born in Brussels, Belgium
- 'Identify your problems, but give your power to solution.' Anthony Robbins (1960–), American motivational speaker, writer and peak performance coach

6 Seven things to do today

- Think about the needs of your company or department, and focus on the strengths you bring to the job to meet those needs.
- Choose one particular skill you bring to the job. Now decide how you can best apply that skill.
- Examine your job description. Is there anything more you can do to make your skills stand out?
- Review your career goals today and again next month. How can this job move you forward? Jot down your thoughts for future reflection.
- If you are facing resistance in your new position, review solutions in the Thursday and Friday chapters and use them.
- Examine any area of weakness or lack of training you have, and decide on options for filling that gap. There may be company-sponsored training, or you may need to train yourself.
- Think about how you'll gain loyalty from your boss and specific colleagues. What can you do to build that loyalty, either by showing loyalty first, or by helping them meet their needs?

7 Seven questions to ask yourself

- Are your assignments in line with what you expected in your new job, based on the interview and job description? If not, clarify this with your boss sooner rather than later.
- Are you willing to do what needs to be done? If not, your attitude and unwillingness can hold you back.
- With regard to new challenges, are you absolutely committed to moving out of your comfort zone to attack hurdles head on?
- If you want to advance in this job, are you doing all you can to fit into the new scene? Consider attitudes, dress code, personal habits and what's expected.
- Are you becoming known for reliability by your timely and consistent follow-up?
- With social media, are you projecting not only who you are today but also who you want to become?
- If you have been hired or promoted to lead, have you mastered the questions to ask to assess changes and engage the team?

Answers

Sunday: 1c; 2d; 3d; 4c; 5d; 6d; 7c; 8d; 9a; 10c.

Monday: 1b; 2c; 3c; 4d; 5a; 6c; 7d; 8d; 9d; 10d.

Tuesday: 1b; 2a; 3b; 4b; 5b; 6d; 7d; 8b; 9b; 10a.

Wednesday: 1d; 2a; 3a; 4b; 5d; 6d; 7a; 8c; 9b; 10d.

Thursday: 1d; 2c; 3d; 4b; 5a; 6b; 7d; 8d; 9a; 10d.

Friday: 1a; 2d; 3b; 4c; 5d; 6a; 7d; 8a; 9d; 10b.

Saturday: 1b; 2d; 3d; 4a; 5a; 6c; 7b; 8d; 9d; 10d.

Notes

ALSO AVAILABLE IN THE 'IN A WEEK' SERIES

APPRAISALS • BRAND MANAGEMENT • BUSINESS PLANS • CONTENT MARKETING • COVER LETTERS • DIGITAL MARKETING • DIRECT MARKETING • EMOTIONAL INTELLIGENCE • FINDING & HIRING TALENT • JOB HUNTING • LEADING TEAMS • MARKET RESEARCH • MARKETING • MBA • MOBILE MARKETING • NETWORKING • OUTSTANDING CONFIDENCE • PEOPLE MANAGEMENT • PLANNING YOUR CAREER • PROJECT MANAGEMENT • SMALL BUSINESS MARKETING • STARTING A NEW JOB • TACKLING TOUGH INTERVIEW QUESTIONS • TIME MANAGEMENT

For information about other titles in the 'In A Week' series, please visit www.teachyourself.co.uk

MORE TITLES AVAILABLE N THE 'IN A WEEK' SERIES

ADVANCED NEGOTIATION SKILLS • ASSERTIVENESS • BUSINESS ECONOMICS • COACHING • COPYWRITING • DECISION MAKING • DIFFICULT CONVERSATIONS • ECOMMERCE • FINANCE FOR NON-FINANCIAL MANAGERS • JOB INTERVIEWS • MANAGING STRESS AT WORK • MANAGING YOUR BOSS • MANAGING YOURSELF • MINDFULNESS AT WORK • NEGOTIATION SKILLS • NLP • PEOPLE SKILLS • PSYCHOMETRIC TESTING • SEO AND SEARCH MARKETING • SOCIAL MEDIA MARKETING • START YOUR OWN BUSINESS • STRATEGY • SUCCESSFUL SELLING • UNDERSTANDING AND INTERPRETING ACCOUNTS

For information about other titles in the 'In A Week' series, please visit www.teachyourself.co.uk

YOUR FASTEST ROUTE TO SUCCESS

LEARN IN A WEEK WHAT THE EXPERTS LEARN IN A LIFETIME

For information about other titles in the 'In A Week' series, please visit www.teachyourself.co.uk